JEWISH THINKERS

General Editor: Arthur Hertzberg

Rashi

Rashi

Chaim Pearl

Grove Press
New York

Copyright © 1988 by Chaim Pearl

Published by Grove Press
a division of Wheatland Corporation
920 Broadway
New York, N.Y. 10010

Library of Congress Cataloging-in-Publication Data

Pearl, Chaim, 1919-
  Rashi / Chaim Pearl.—1st ed.
    p. cm.—(Jewish thinkers)
  Bibliography: p.
  Includes index.
  ISBN 0-8021-1063-0
  1. Rashi, 1040-1105. 2. Rabbis—France—Biography.
3. Scholars, Jewish—France—Biography. I. Title. II. Series.
BM755.S6P4 1988
296.1'092'4—dc 19
[B]   88-4564
                                                       CIP
              680 65836
Manufactured in the United States of America
First Edition 1988
10 9 8 7 6 5 4 3 2 1

.sH

CONTENTS

Note on Transliteration

The general system of transliteration has been used. The dot under the H has been included to denote the Hebrew letter *chet* and has been used where essential to pronunciation or meaning. A superior comma has been used to denote the Hebrew letters *aleph* and *ayin*, e.g. Ba'al.

France, Provence and the Rhineland

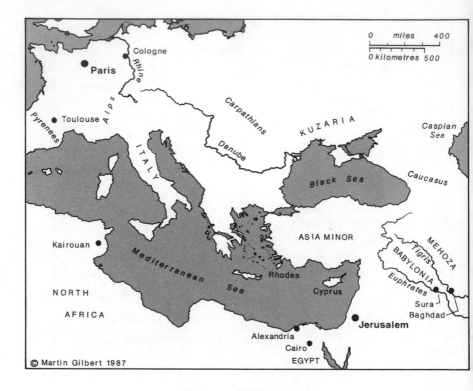

Scale:
0   miles   400
0 kilometres 500

Paris

Cologne

Rhine

Alps

Toulouse

Pyrenees

Carpathians

KUZARIA

Caspian
Sea

ITALY

Danube

Black Sea

Caucasus

Kairouan

Mediterranean

ASIA MINOR

MEHOZA

Tigris

BABYLONIA

Euphrates

Sea

Rhodes

Cyprus

Sura

Baghdad

NORTH

AFRICA

Jerusalem

Alexandria

Cairo

EGYPT

© Martin Gilbert 1987

Europe and Western Asia

INTRODUCTION

Among the names of the greatest Jewish teachers the name of Rabbi Solomon ben Isaac—Rashi—stands out as one of the most distinguished of all time. His fame rests on two monumental works, his commentary on the Bible and his commentary on the Talmud.

Bible commentary and interpretation is almost as old as the earliest Jewish communities in ancient Israel. Prophets, priests and levites all interpreted the word of God to the people to make its sense clear. The return of the Jews from Babylonian exile in the fifth century BCE inaugurated a period of even more intense activity in the field of biblical interpretation. In subsequent ages the rabbis were basically involved in a detailed examination of the Bible text in order to expose its fullest meaning. This work was continued throughout the ages; in fact right up to our own time, with modern scholars bringing to our attention the insights gained from the new sciences of archeology, comparative religion, linguistics and history. Bible commentary is thus an activity which has never been absent from the Jewish scene, from earliest times to the present.

The most famous as well as the most important Bible commentary ever written is that of the eleventh-century French teacher Rashi. Its greatness lies in the unique Rashi method, in which the scholar provides the Bible reader with the plain meaning of the text and also introduces him at the same time to the deeper religious and ethical teachings which lie below the surface and which he quotes from the treasury of rabbinic sources. The reader is thus twice blessed in that he reaches an understanding of the text and also gathers up the traditional wisdom of the rabbinic exposition. All this Rashi does in his beautifully clear and concise literary style.

His second work, the commentary on the Talmud, is in some respects even more outstanding. The language of the Talmud is difficult. Its style is frequently dense and its subject matter is complicated. Rashi seems to face all these and other problems with an extraordinary poise and equilibrium. He simply gets on with his job of explaining the difficult text and bringing clarity and enlightenment to the talmudic discourse. It is likely that without Rashi's brilliant commentary the Talmud would have remained a virtually neglected work. It was he who paved the way in making the Talmud, next to the Bible, the foundation of Jewish life and thought.

Students of the Bible and Talmud never fail to read the original texts together with Rashi's commentary, so that the master commentator's explanations and insights go hand in hand with the text. Rabbi Solomon ben Isaac lived nine hundred years ago; but his influence on Jewish learning has never abated in all that time. Indeed, with the modern heightened interest in Jewish study, it can be truthfully said that Rashi's influence today is as deep as it ever was.

This book starts with an account of the historical background of eleventh-century French Jewry, as well as with the story of Rashi's life. It then goes on to examine in some detail Rashi's Bible commentary with some examples of his method and style. In a further chapter we examine Rashi's Talmud commentary, again with some illustrative examples of his method. Finally we shall survey the extraordinary influence of Rashi's work from the time that he wrote until our own day.

It is hoped that readers of this book will gain from it an understanding of Rashi's permanent and creative contribution to the history of Bible and Talmud scholarship, and will realize why he is acclaimed as one of the greatest teachers in Jewish history.

I

HISTORICAL BACKGROUND

I

The history of the Jews in ancient France goes back as far as the third century, by which time there were already small groups in various parts of the country as well as in some cities of the Rhine. It is likely that members of these earliest settlements followed the Roman armies into Gaul: some of them may have even served as soldiers in those armies. The records show that there were Jews in Metz, Avignon, Arles, Brittany, Narbonne and Orleans, as well as in the Rhenish cities of Mainz and Cologne. These communities were all very small until about the ninth century when they began to increase with immigration from Babylon, Italy and Spain.

Until the First Crusade, at the end of the eleventh century, the French Jewish community lived in conditions of virtual freedom from serious restrictions, and the rulers of the country were remarkably tolerant towards the Jews of their kingdom. Charlemagne (747–814), the founder of the Frankish empire, was noted for his favourable attitude towards them. He even included a Jew, a certain Isaac, in the delegation he sent to the Caliph Harun al Rashid, and when Isaac returned from Baghdad he brought with him an elephant from the caliph to the French king.

Louis the Pious (778–840) was even more kindly disposed towards the Jews. In Lyons the authorities changed the market day from a Saturday to a weekday in order to make it possible for the Jews to participate.

In January 1074 the Emperor Henry IV (1050–1106) exempted all the citizens of Worms from poll tax, in recognition of their loyalty. The inclusion of the Jews in the royal ordinance is an indication of their happy status within the general society in which they lived at this time. He also gave the Jews of Speyer his personal protection: they were granted virtual autonomy and could settle all their disputes in conformity with Jewish law. The Bishop of Speyer had announced earlier, 'Desiring to make a town out of the village of Speyer, I thought to raise its dignity many times by getting Jews to settle there' and soon after Henry gave privileges to the Jews of Speyer the same were granted to the Jews of Worms. However, this may have been no more than confirmation of a situation which had already existed under previous monarchs.

In their economic life the Jews also enjoyed great freedom and even prosperity. There were a few physicians and even some sailors, but most of them were merchants. They imported and exported a variety of goods and counted non-Jews as well as fellow Jews among their customers. There were also some skilled artisans who worked in coin stamping, blacksmithing, metal work and glass work. They were allowed to own buildings, real estate, farms and orchards, and so there were also Jewish farmers and keepers of bees and livestock.

Beyond this wide range of activity, Jews were especially noted as vintners, particularly during the tenth and eleventh centuries. At one stage they virtually monopolized the market, and even wine for the Christian Mass was bought from them. The Jewish vintners often worked their vineyards themselves. Indeed, the rather strict regulations which prohibited Jews from using wine handled by Gentiles would have necessitated a great deal of personal involvement from the Jewish vintner in the winemaking process, especially in its later stages.

With characteristic diligence, a few Jews advanced to positions of some distinction. Among them could be found purveyors to the imperial court, collectors of taxes, ambassadors to kings and even Church administrators.

In addition, relations with the Gentile community were cordial. Throughout this period, and in all Jewish communities of Northern France and the Rhineland, Jews dressed the same as their Gentile neighbours: they spoke the same languages and both groups joined in happy as well as sad civic occasions. When

Archbishop Bardoe of Mainz died in 1051 the Jews came to pay their respects. They bowed before the prelate's coffin and placed ashes on their heads as a token of mourning. Jews and Christians took note of each other's sacred feasts and fasts and we have an account of Jews receiving gifts of permitted foods from their Christian neighbours after the Passover Festival. Above all there was close interaction between Jewish merchants and their Gentile clients. They lent money to each other, sometimes on trust, without any formal pledge. This closeness frequently led to friendly personal relationships.

It is only fair to state, however, that the attitude of the Christian clergy appears at times somewhat ambiguous. There were some sporadic attempts to convert the Jews. Perhaps it was precisely on account of the cordial relationships between members of the two communities that Church leaders attempted now and then to restrict contact between Jew and Christian. Thus they objected to Jews and Christians dining together, Jews were discouraged from going out of their houses during the Easter Festival, and in some places they were not allowed to have Christian servants. It is not easy to discover the extent to which these Church laws were observed, nor indeed when and for how long they were promulgated: in fact the records show that it was general practice for Jews to employ non-Jewish servants in their homes. We know, of course, that in its official teachings the Church unquestionably maintained its anti-Jewish doctrines. However, it is also clear that at least until the First Crusade the Jews of France enjoyed a period of harmonious relationships with their neighbours in which there was an absence of any significant persecution or Jew hatred.

It was Rashi's good fortune, and the good fortune of the Jewish people, that he lived nearly all his life in a time when conditions for Jews in the Franco-German lands were good. Some of the greatest and most creative masterpieces of Jewish literature were produced against a background of relative stability, by people who had the opportunity to live in comparative peace, for example, much of the Babylonian Talmud and the great philosophical works of medieval Spain during its so-called Golden Age. Rashi's monumental work, too, was accomplished at a time when the social, political and economic situation of the Jews was relatively stable. It is tempting to suggest that, at the least, these favourable conditions permitted him to devote all his time to, and to concentrate all his intellectual powers on, producing works which have remained among the most cherished spiritual legacies of the Jewish people.

II

The foregoing brief historical sketch touches only on the social and economic life of French Jewry. But our chief interest in this study is the life and work of one of the greatest Jewish scholars of all time. It is hardly likely that anyone can produce a monumental work of scholarship in a community which is intellectually barren: the likelihood is that there exists some appropriate background against which the work is nurtured. Sure enough, Rashi's great work appears within a framework of a society which pursued Jewish learning. The tone was set by his distinguished predecessors.

In one important respect the scholarly activity of Jews in Franco-German lands was unique. This is best seen if we compare it to the medieval Spanish Jewish community. There, the main emphasis was on Jewish philosophy and poetry. It is generally conceded that the time and the place contributed to that. Jewish religious philosophy was systematized and expounded for the first time as a result of the rival claims of the Church on the one hand and of Islam on the other. Judah Halevi (c. 1075–1141), the famous Spanish Jewish poet and philosopher, who lived at about the same time as Rashi, actually sets down his philosophical exposition of Judaism in a book called the *Kuzari*, employing the dramatic background of the Jewish teacher who has to represent Judaism in the face of the rival claims of the other two faiths. In a sense, the Jewish teachers had to provide their own answers to these claims, and this demand produced a long line of important works on Jewish philosophy, written over a period of some four hundred years. There was no similar influence at work in France, where Islam had no hold and the power of the Church was exercised less aggressively than in

Spain. Jewish poetry in Spain was also influenced by the Arab poets, and the friendliness which existed at that particular time between the Jews and the Moors undoubtedly stirred Jewish poetic creativity. Nothing like it existed in France to affect Jewish writing, and what poetry there was was confined to liturgical hymns, mostly written after the Crusades.

In one respect however the medieval community in Franco-Germany excelled over the Spanish community—in the field of biblical exegesis, and more particularly in Talmud study.

The great centre for the study of the Talmud had been Babylon. It was there that for almost seven centuries the eminent teachers and respected authorities of rabbinic law converged in order to expound and to codify the vast corpus of Jewish Oral Law. The historic academies of Sura, Pumpeditha, Mehoza and Nehardea produced hundreds of distinguished scholars and teachers as well as creating a vital ambience for a learned laity. Scholarship—and particularly talmudic scholarship—was the prestigious pursuit of Babylonian Jewry which culminated in the compilation of the massive Babylonian Talmud in the year 500 CE. But the work of the scholars of Babylon did not cease at that point: subsequent generations of interpreters continued with the talmudic scholarly tradition and added considerably to the depth and extent of rabbinic post-talmudic literature. This activity went on almost to the end of the tenth century.

Persecution, first from the Zoroastrians and then from the more militant Muslims, but particularly the divisions within the Jewish community itself, weakened the once proud, wealthy and distinguished Babylonian Jewry. The religious and lay leadership was not replaced; academies closed and were not reopened; the end was inevitable. But new communities with a new and brilliant scholarly leadership had begun to emerge among the Jews of Spain and Franco-Germany.

The Franco-German communities were well established by the beginning of the eleventh century, in relative peace and prosperity. New immigrants were arriving in increasing numbers. They journeyed to the Italian peninsula and from there they made their way to all parts of France and the Rhineland. Merchants had their own motivation for travel and they found the peaceful conditions of life conducive to their success. Scholars brought with them the dedication of the old Babylonian academies and in that spirit they established new centres of rabbinic learning. They attracted disciples from all over the Franco-German lands and managed to rebuild the closed Babylonian academies on new soil.

The greatest rabbinic leader in the pre-Rashi period was Gershom of Mainz (960–1028). Born in Metz, he established his academy in Mainz where he continued to teach for the remainder of his life. Gershom exercised great rabbinic authority over European Jewry by both his scholarship and his qualities of leadership. His special *takkanot*, or new ordinances, generally promulgated at rabbinical assemblies, were accepted as authoritative and binding on all European Jewry. Two of the most important *takkanot* associated with his name dealt with the status of the woman in Jewish law. The first one ruled that, in spite of the biblical permissibility, bigamy was outlawed and could no longer be practised by a Jew. The second important *takkanah* modified the biblical laws of divorce. According to the Bible it is only the husband who takes the initiative in a divorce proceeding. He has the document of divorce written and delivered to his wife whether or not she is a consenting party. Rabbenu Gershom's *takkanah* ruled that divorce can be effected only with the consent of both parties: the husband must willingly have the document of divorce written and the wife must be willing to accept it.

One of the greatest achievements of Rabbenu Gershom was to collate a complete and authentic text of the Talmud. It should be remembered that in the days before the invention of printing, texts of the Talmud, and even of the Bible, were very rare and extremely expensive. Most of the teaching was therefore conducted orally, usually with only the teacher possessing a copy of the text he was teaching. Students, scholars and scribes copied out the text for themselves. There was therefore always the possibility of a copyist making an error in transcribing the text, or even of someone deliberately emending the text in the belief that what he had in front of him was incorrect. Thus there arose a variety of readings of the same passage, with the later problem of deciding which was authentic.

In the case of the Bible this was not so serious since an accepted *Masorah*, or tradition, already existed, which authenticated every word of the Bible. There was no question of deliberate alteration, only the possibility of simple human error. Gershom also undertook to make known his complete Bible text which was correct to the last detail of the *Masorah*.

The problem with the Talmud was far more difficult, first, because its literature is far more voluminous than the Bible, secondly, because, as we have noted, variant readings already existed. That left the scholar with the riddle of deciding which was the correct or the original text. To any student of the Talmud, the matter was of first importance. Rabbenu Gershom was responsible for putting together a complete manuscript of the Talmud bearing his signature. His copy contained what he believed was the authentic text and therefore he discouraged all others from making any emendations. Such a cautionary warning was necessary, for by this time the number of Talmud students and scholars had increased, with the rise of talmudic studies all over Lorraine. In this way, Gershom's text became, more or less, the accepted and authentic text of the Talmud, and it is believed that Rashi used it in his great work which we shall be discussing later.

Gershom's eminence as a scholar and his acknowledged authority gained for him the description *Maor Hagolah*—The Light of the Exile. This title of distinction apparently derives from a reference to him in a Responsum which Rashi wrote some years later, in which he says, 'Rabbenu Gershom has enlightened the eyes of the Captivity, for all live by his instruction. All the Jews of these countries call themselves the disciples of his disciples.' Indeed, Rashi himself was just that—a disciple of Gershom's disciples. (He himself was to earn such a title of distinction: his later followers called themselves 'the disciples of Rashi's disciples'.) Among the outstanding students of Rabbenu Gershom were Jacob ben Yakar and Isaac ben Judah. These two were among Rashi's own teachers.

2

THE LIFE OF RASHI

I

The name Rashi is made up of three Hebrew letters, *resh, shin, yod*, which are the abbreviations for Rabbi Shlomo Yitzhaki or Rabbi Solomon the son of Isaac. The great scholar mostly signed his name Shlomo Yitzhaki or just with the two-letter abbreviation Shai (*shin* and *yod*). His disciples frequently referred to him as *Rabbenu* or *Hamoreh*—Our Teacher. Two hundred years or so after his death, some Christian scholars misinterpreted the name Rashi as the mnemonic for Rabbi Shlomo Hayarhi, implying that he was born in the city 'of the moon', i.e. Lunel, but all the accepted evidence points to his birthplace as Troyes in north-eastern France, not far from the border with Germany.

Everyone agrees that Rashi died in 1105, and there is even a record of the exact date of his death—Thursday 29 Tammuz 4865. This corresponds with 13 July 1105. There is a tradition that he was sixty-five when he died, which would make the year of his birth 1040, but some scholars have doubted whether anyone could have achieved as much as Rashi did in a lifespan of sixty-five years. They therefore prefer an earlier date for Rashi's birth, some of them putting it at 1030. A third tradition has it that Rashi was born in the year that Rabbenu Gershom died, i.e. 1028. However, in the absence of any firm evidence to the contrary, there is no reason why we should depart from the accepted tradition that Rashi was born in 1040.

At that time France was divided into about twelve provinces, each ruled by a local count or duke. Troyes, the city of Rashi's birth, was the capital of Champagne in northern France. It was on the main trade route connecting Italy with France and then on to the North Sea. Because of its proximity to Germany it had close contacts with all the cities of Lorraine and Germany itself, so it was able to maintain its place as an important commercial centre in Franco-German lands up to the end of the fourteenth century. Twice a year there were important trade fairs in Troyes which attracted merchants, Jews as well as non-Jews, from all over France, from Germany and even from England and Italy. There are still ancient street names in modern Troyes which recall the medieval trades which were once practised there— Great Tannery Street, Small Tannery Street, Goldsmiths' Street and Money Street. In his commentaries Rashi shows familiarity with those trades and with many others which he apparently knew from personal visits to the places of work.

The Jewish community of Troyes was not large, perhaps not more than a hundred families. This was not unusual; with the exception of a few cities, all the medieval Jewish communities in the country were relatively small. Most of the Jews in eleventh-century Troyes were merchants; others were artisans and there was a fair proportion who owned land. They lived under the benevolent rule of the counts, some of whom extended to the Jews their personal protection. The count of Champagne in Rashi's time was Theobald I.

Very little is known about Rashi's early childhood. In fact, it has been suggested that, as in his voluminous writings his father is hardly mentioned, there is reason to believe that Isaac, the father, must have died in Rashi's childhood.[1] In one source Rashi's father is referred to as a *kadosh*, a martyr, and there is a possibility that in some unknown circumstances he suffered a martyr's fate. But this is very unlikely as we would then expect some definite reference to the fact in Rashi's own writings. However, it is very often the case that, when historical facts are unavailable, popular folk legend tries to fill in the gaps. We will tell some of these stories, not because they have any historical basis but because they are of intrinsic value as part of a collection of Rashi legends. Further, the very fact that they were told and popularized illustrates the love of the masses for Rashi.

The first legend is about Isaac, Rashi's father, who is described in the story as a dealer in precious stones. Isaac once

9

possessed a very special jewel which was desired by the local bishop to adorn a figure of the Virgin Mary in his church. The cleric sent his agents to buy the stone from Isaac, but when the latter learned of the purpose for which it was intended he refused to sell the jewel, thinking that to do so would be an act of disloyalty to his own faith. The church messengers offered more money, but Isaac remained firm in his refusal to sell. Finally the bishop's men departed to report their failure. On receiving their disappointing report the bishop decided that, having failed to obtain the jewel fairly, he would take it by foul means. So a few days later he sent other men with the story that there was a wealthy merchant on the other side of the river who was interested in buying the stone. The men looked genuine enough, so Isaac took the jewel and went with them into their boat to meet with the 'customer'. When they were in the middle of the river the men pounced on him and demanded that he surrender the jewel to be delivered to the church. Seeing that he had been tricked, Isaac took the jewel out of his pocket and dropped it overboard, where it immediately sank and was lost for ever. The legend concludes that Isaac then heard a heavenly voice which announced, 'Isaac, because you have sacrificed a precious jewel for the honour of your faith, you will be granted a jewel of a son whose brilliance will illuminate Jewish life and thought for all time.' Isaac and his wife had been childless for ten years; and within that year Rashi was born.

A second legend tells of an incident involving Rashi's mother, who was then in an advanced stage of pregnancy. One day, while she was walking down a narrow lane in Troyes, the driver of a cart lost control of the horse, which galloped furiously towards the spot where Rashi's mother was. At the last moment, and just before the uncontrolled animal could run her down, the frightened woman pressed herself against the wall which miraculously gave way to allow her to remain safely in the niche until the vehicle had passed her. The legend goes on to tell that the same niche could be seen for many years afterwards as a visible testimony to the miraculous intervention of the Divine Providence in the birth of Rashi. In the same genre of fantastic stories we may note the tradition that, years later, a butcher set up his shop in the house where Rashi was born. Strange to tell, it is reported, no fly ever appeared in that shop. The story is, of course, reminiscent of a similar legend about the Temple butchery area which was also free of flies.

An interesting legend relates to the time when, as a wandering scholar, Rashi went to Toledo to visit Judah Halevi, the Spanish Jewish philosopher and poet. Halevi of course was about thirty years younger than Rashi, but this did not prevent the French scholar from seeking out his Spanish colleague. At the time of his visit Halevi was not at home and Rashi left. But on his departure the servants discovered that a fine silk coat was missing. They pursued Rashi and caught up with him. Rashi's protests notwithstanding, he was made to pay for the coat. But before leaving the house he wrote on the door the Hebrew word *Shlomo* five times. When Judah Halevi returned home his servants told him what had happened and they were immediately ordered to find Rashi and bring him back to the house. They soon found the by now penniless Rashi in the schoolhouse. He was brought back and treated by his host as an honoured guest. Of course the money was returned to him and Rashi prepared to leave. But first Halevi asked the meaning of his strange writing on the door. Rashi took a piece of paper and punctuated the five words as follows: *shelama shlomo salma shelama shilma?*—'Why did Solomon have to pay for your beautiful coat?'

Folklore goes on to tell that on one of his journeys Rashi, who was familiar with medicine, saved the life of a Christian monk. The Jewish scholar would take no reward, but asked the monk to be of help to persecuted Jews whenever he could. Some years later the same monk, now an official of the Papal Office, interceded with the Pope to save the Jews of Prague from what would have been a devastating pogrom.

Now let us leave legend and return to historical facts. Although history records nothing about Rashi's father, we know that his mother came from a scholarly family and that her brother was Rabbi Simeon ben Isaac the Elder, the author of several pieces of liturgical poetry.[2]

It is believed that Rashi was married when he was seventeen or eighteen. He had two daughters, Miriam and Jochabed, who married students of their father: Miriam married Judah ben Nathan and had a son, Yomtob, and a daughter; Jochabed married Meir ben Samuel and had four sons and one daughter. The sons were named Samuel, Isaac, Jacob and Solomon, who was born after Rashi's death. They all became famous scholars and achieved great distinction on their own merit: we shall have need to say something about them later.

On the basis of a letter sent by Jacob, the son of Rashi's daughter Jochabed, to his cousin Yomtob, some biographers refer to a third daughter who was married to a certain Eliezer and divorced. Jacob writes of the divorce of their *dodah* or aunt, referring to her and her divorced husband by their French names, Belle Assez and Jocelyn. In the tradition, her Hebrew name was Rachel. However, it should be remembered that *dodah* might loosely mean a cousin rather than an aunt.

Rashi received his early education in Worms from Isaac Halevi. There exists a small chapel in that city which is called Rashi's Chapel, and is traditionally the site of the place where Rashi studied and taught. However, although it was for long venerated as a site associated with Rashi's life and work, the chapel was built many years after Rashi's death. During the German occupation in the Second World War the building was destroyed. It was rebuilt in 1950.

Rashi knew that to further his knowledge of Talmud he would have to go to Mainz, then the greatest centre of talmudic study, so after his marriage he spent some years in the academy established by the famous Rabbenu Gershom studying under Gershom's own disciples, Jacob ben Yakar and Isaac ben Judah. Rashi acknowledged his great debt to his teachers: 'Indeed I grew from a great tree, Rabbi Jacob ben Yakar . . . at all events my heart and outlook and understanding come from him.' At the same time his teachers showered great praise on the distinguished disciple and even sent to him some of their own questions on Jewish law.

Rashi lived as a poor student, and his passionate search for an ever deeper understanding of the sacred texts was not adversely affected by his family responsibilities. Legend also follows him during his years as a wandering scholar. On completing his education in Mainz, folklore describes him as travelling to distant lands in order to seek out the most eminent Jewish teachers. He is said to have journeyed to Italy, Greece, Egypt, Palestine and Spain, whence the legend of his meeting with Judah Halevi.

Finally he returned to his native city of Troyes and started his own academy which soon attracted students from all over the country. At the time of his return, Rashi was about twenty-five years old, and he was appointed to serve as a rabbinic judge in the community. He did not receive any remuneration for his rabbinic duties (the office of professional rabbi was unknown until many years later): like all other rabbis and teachers he earned his living from other work. Thus, one of Rashi's grandsons, Samuel, owned a herd of cattle, and another, Jacob, was a moneylender and for a time a government tax agent. Rashi himself owned vineyards. It is reported that he inherited the property from the estate of a wealthy woman vintner. Fortunately, his work gave him ample time to attend to his life's real work—the massive commentaries on the Bible and Talmud.

The last years of Rashi's life were saddened by the events of the First Crusade which was organized in 1095. In the spring and summer of the following year, ignorant and murderous mobs joined the armies of the Cross to wrest the Holy Sepulchre and other sites sacred to Christianity from the possession of the Muslims. On their way to the Holy Land their route passed through many cities of the Rhineland where Jewish communities had lived peacefully for many centuries. The crusading soldiers thought it senseless to march thousands of miles to do battle with one infidel, while on their very doorstep were the Jewish infidels—the ones who had killed Jesus. In their inflamed bloodthirstiness and lust for easy loot they ravished the helpless Jewish communities, and left them desolate. Thousands of innocent men, women and children were massacred. The 'gallant soldiers of the Cross' robbed, raped and murdered eight hundred Jews in the city of Worms and thirteen hundred in Mainz. A similar fate befell the Jews of Treves, Speyer and Cologne. Many of those who survived were able to do so only by agreeing to be baptized.

This fact led to some controversy later on. After the crusading armies had passed through their territory, many of those who had saved their lives by accepting baptism then wished to return to Judaism and the synagogue, but some members of the community did not take too kindly to the return of the apostates, however superficial their apostasy had been. In this matter, just as Maimonides did about a hundred years later in similar circumstances, Rashi showed a liberal spirit, an understanding of human nature, and a warm sympathy for those who had sought life at the price of agreeing to be sprinkled with the holy water of the Church. His tolerant attitude is illustrated by the following Responsum: 'Let us beware of alienating those who have returned to us by repulsing them. They became Christians only through fear of death; and as soon as the danger disappeared they hastened to return to their faith.'

Troyes itself remained physically unmolested by the First Crusade, but the events in the cities of the Rhine were close enough to affect the Jews of northern France. They knew what was happening to their brethren not far away and Rashi was particularly sensitive to the disasters which had befallen his colleagues, his disciples and the great centres of Jewish learning with their scholars. Some comments of Rashi on the Psalms and other books of the Bible seem to have been written against the dark background of Jewish suffering during that time. Thus, on the verse *For all day have I been plagued, and my chastisement came every morning* (Ps. 73:14), Rashi commented: 'It appears that every day—from one morning till the next—fresh troubles fall on us.' On the verse *For I am ready to halt and every pain is continually before me* (Ps. 38:18) Rashi says, 'We are sadly experienced in sufferings and are always on the point of being destroyed.' Reference to the story of the suffering of the Jews during the Crusades is probably intended in Rashi's comment on Psalm 38:1, *A Psalm of David to make memorial*, when he observes, 'This psalm is to be read in a time of tribulation when the Holy One Blessed be He can be "reminded" of the suffering of all the Jewish people.' Certainly, the anguish expressed in the psalm will have symbolized for Rashi the cry of pain of the Jewish communities savagely attacked by the Crusaders. In the next Psalm, 39:2–5, Rashi again reads the psalmist's personal quest for God's justice as the agonizing search of the people as a whole to understand the meaning of their suffering in the light of their belief in Divine justice.

Of special interest is Rashi's treatment of the 'suffering servant' passage in Isaiah 53. The Church reads this chapter as a prophecy concerning Jesus, who suffered for the sins of mankind, a reading which was, of course, unacceptable to the Jews, who saw the chapter as a pointed description of Jewish suffering in their exile. Rashi sees the chapter in this light, but also relates the theme to the persecution of the Jews in his time. Let us see for example his treatment of Isaiah 53:9: *And they made his grave with the wicked, and with the rich his tomb; although he had done no violence, neither was any deceit in his mouth.* Rashi commented: 'They murdered the exiled Jew just as they murdered the wicked. Although he [the Jew] was perfectly innocent they treated him as a villain. Moreover, the innocent Jew delivered himself up to his persecutors who would have left him alone had he denied his religion and converted. The reference to the death of the rich illustrates that the enemy killed the Jew because of his property and not because of any crime of which he was accused. They also employed different kinds of execution for the victims; some were burned, others were stoned, and others killed in different ways. But all the victims were martyred.' Rashi here wrote with the tragic events of the Crusaders' massacres very much in his mind.

A curious legend associates Rashi with Godfrey of Bouillon, one of the leaders of the First Crusade. He heard of the wisdom of the Jewish sage and, wishing to consult him about his chances of returning victorious from the battles with the Muslims in the Holy Land, sent messengers to Troyes who commanded Rashi in their master's name to appear before him. Rashi, however, refused, whereupon Godfrey himself went to Troyes and arrived at Rashi's academy to face the rabbi in person. But he found the place quite empty and Rashi nowhere to be seen. The Christian knight called out for him but still Rashi did not appear. Finally Godfrey called, 'Come forth, and I give you my solemn promise that no harm will come to you.' Rashi then came out of hiding and stood before Godfrey.

'What is it you want?' asked the sage.

'I want you to tell me if I will succeed in my mission, and if I will return safely with my army,' said the Crusader.

'At first you will succeed,' answered Rashi. 'But your enemies will finally destroy your army, and you will return here with only two horsemen.'

Godfrey was outraged at the rabbi's words and angrily said, 'Know this for a certainty, that if I come back with but one more horse and its rider you will be executed and the Jews of France will be put to the sword.'

The Crusader left for the Holy Land and fought there for several years. At first he succeeded, and the Holy Sepulchre fell into Christian hands. In addition to killing many followers of Islam, the record tells that he also massacred the Jews of Jerusalem in the summer of 1098. But then, just as Rashi had foretold, Godfrey's armies were routed and destroyed. In fact, he himself died there, but legend tells that he made his sad way back and arrived at the gates of Troyes with three horsemen. Remembering Rashi's prophecy he was determined to carry out his warning, but as he rode under the gate of the city a heavy stone fell on one of his men killing both horse and rider. Thus, Rashi's prophecy was fulfilled to the end. The Crusader was so moved by this that he wanted to visit Rashi with the intention this time of paying his respects, but by then the Jewish teacher had died.

The tragic events of the First Crusade probably affected Rashi's health and towards the end of his life he was too weak to write. He dictated Responsa on questions of Jewish law to his grandsons and his friends. But, fortunately for Jewish history, by that time Rashi's monumental work on the Bible and Talmud was all but completed. He finished his work on the whole of the Bible, with the exception of the Book of Chronicles. With regard to the Talmud commentary, part of tractate Baba Batra (from page 29a) was completed by Rashi's grandson, Samuel ben Meir, and one or two of the other tractates were finished by others. The last writing of Rashi himself is found in tractate

Makkoth, where his commentary went up to page 19b. The remaining pages were written by his son-in-law, Judah ben Nathan, the husband of Rashi's daughter Miriam. Rashi himself finished his work on that book with an explanation on purity, and Judah took up his pen and wrote, 'Here our master of pure body, his soul expiring in purity, ceased commenting. From here on it is the language of his pupil Judah ben Nathan.'

II

Thus ended the life of one of the most remarkable scholars in Jewish history. We will be considering the extent of his massive contribution to Jewish intellectual life and how he brought an understanding of the Bible and Talmud to layman and scholar. The Bible, particularly the Pentateuch, was read by all Jews, and Rashi's commentaries opened up for them the meaning of the text and a deeper appreciation of its profound teaching. The Talmud was not study material for the average layman, but the student of Judaism and the scholar needed to come to grips with its text, an understanding of which was crucial to the understanding of Judaism, and, as we shall see, the Talmud would long have remained a closed book without Rashi's explanation of that difficult work.

In addition to his monumental commentaries on the Bible and Talmud, Rashi is the author of several other works dealing mainly with legal matters. These are the *Sefer Pardes, Sefer Ha'Orah* and *Siddur Rashi*. It is believed that the actual writing of these works was done by his disciples, but with his full knowledge and even his instruction. Above all, the most important of these works is a collection of about three hundred and fifty Responsa. The significance of this class of writing is relevant to our account of Rashi's life.

The Responsa literature belongs to a genre of writing which is of great importance in the history of Jewish law from the post-talmudic period. Questions on Jewish law and life were addressed to recognized scholars who considered the questions in the light of precedent, past decisions, current opinion and the realities of contemporary life. Hundreds of rabbis from about the eighth century—even to our own day—have written many thousands of Responsa on every kind of question, addressed to them by Jews from communities all over the world. In the Middle Ages, Jewish merchants and scholars were great travellers and they served as the unofficial but well trusted postmen who delivered the written questions to the authority on Jewish law to whom they were addressed and would gladly pass on the expert's written replies. In this way an active correspondence was maintained by individuals and communities in Babylon, North Africa, Spain, Italy, France and Germany. Rashi's correspondence was somewhat more restricted, to Responsa to individuals and communities in France and the Rhineland cities.

The Responsa literature is fascinating for several other reasons. It is not only important for our understanding of the history of Jewish law, but it frequently casts light on the history and social conditions of a Jewish community in the Middle Ages and so it is important for a deeper understanding of the social history of those communities. Further, more often than not, the question and its answer gives us a glimpse into the standards of Jewish religious observance prevalent in that place and at that time. Finally, the Responsa works are interesting in that they give us a picture of the personality and character of the teacher concerned. Is he sympathetic or insensitive, lenient or strict? Does he show modesty, friendliness and concern?

Rashi's Responsa are especially valuable from this point of view, because we not only get a statement of his opinions on the law which is the subject of the question; we also obtain from his communication a clearer picture of his personality. This is all the more important when we have regard to the fact that in his major works—the commentaries—Rashi does not speak much about himself: only very rarely does he allow the student of the commentaries to glimpse the writer. Of course, even here we can get some idea of his character and attitudes; but it is not enough. A much fuller and clearer picture of Rashi's character is derived from his correspondence, which becomes all the more interesting when we want to discover what kind of man he was.

What stands out in this correspondence are Rashi's qualities of kindliness, gentleness and humility. His liberal spirit is also amply in evidence. In one letter he states that it is no sin if a man interrupts his Grace after Meals in order to feed his animals, because the Torah itself commands us to feed our beasts before we ourselves partake of food. In another Responsum he writes to a man who has sent him a question without signing his name: 'I recognize the author of the letter from his writing. He was afraid to sign his name because he suspects that I am hostile to him. But I want to assure him that I am not, and have quite the opposite feelings towards him.'[3]

He tells how once, when he was a student, in the house of his teacher he noticed that a dietary law was being broken in the preparation of some meat. His teacher was present at the time, but was busy with another matter. The young Rashi was in a quandary. To say nothing would be to permit the meat to be prepared in a way that was against the law. On the other hand, to intervene in the matter would be disrespectful to his teacher, and a disciple was always discouraged from offering an opinion on the law while his master was present. Rashi showed great common sense, tact and presence of mind by asking his teacher a question bearing on the issue which he witnessed.[4]

Another reported incident illustrates the same quality of tact and common sense. When he was a student in Worms, a non-Jew delivered wine to a Jew. The question was asked whether the Jew could use the wine which had been handled by a Gentile. Rashi's teacher, Jacob ben Yakar, withdrew from the study hall so as not to become involved. But Rashi would not pass an opinion, and he ran after his teacher with the question about the permissibility of using the wine.[5]

This does not mean that he lacked independence of mind. Much as he revered his teachers, Rashi sometimes disagreed with their opinions. In such situations he said so, but he offered his view with great circumspection and would not try to change practices founded on his teachers' instruction until he became totally convinced that an error had been made.

Rashi showed himself to be a very humble scholar. Rarely dogmatic, he was always ready to acknowledge that he himself may have made a mistake or that he did not know the answer to a problem. In one Responsum he wrote, 'The same question has already been put to me, and I gave a faulty answer. But now I am convinced of my mistake, and I am prepared to give a decision based on sounder reason.' There are numerous places in both his Bible and Talmud commentaries where the humble Rashi admits that he does not understand the meaning of the text. This is perhaps unique among medieval commentators.[6]

A similar modesty is found in many places in his commentaries where Rashi admits that he had no knowledge or understanding of the matter in question.[7] Thus, commenting on Zechariah 11:13, he admits, 'I have seen many interpretations of this prophecy which I cannot understand.' We read how he was reluctant to make decisions for Jews of another community outside his own. He once said, 'What am I that I should consider myself an authority in other places... I am a man of little importance, and my hands are feeble... ' His grandson Rashbam (Samuel ben Meir) wrote that his grandfather admitted to him that he had made some mistakes and only lack of time prevented him from revising all his work.[8] This modesty, combined with a passionate search for the truth, are the qualities of a genuine scholar and a truly great man.

Rashi's liberal tendencies are also in evidence in his correspondence. As can be well imagined, his Responsa dealt with a very wide variety of subjects—from a rule in Hebrew grammar to a question on the meaning of a passage in the Bible or Talmud; from a question about the liturgy to the difficult problem of the proper attitude to be shown to apostates wishing to return to the Jewish community. In a matter of ritual law he also exhibits a lenient approach. He is aware of the weakness of those who take the easier way out by being strict in ritual matters rather than searching for a reason to be more lenient. He said, 'The authority of those who prohibit without cause means little; for anyone can hand down a prohibition even in matters that are permissible.'[9]

His love for his fellow man was strong enough to overrule an accepted ritual practice. Thus, on one occasion, when a death occurred during the Intermediate Days of a festival, there was an opinion—based on the prevalent custom—that certain prayers be omitted in deference to the joyous spirit of the festival. Rashi felt that to do so would detract from the respect due to the deceased and the bereaved family, so he recited those prayers. On returning from the funeral he went to the house of the mourners to comfort them and he even offered a eulogy to the deceased, beginning by saying that it was difficult for him to sit there in silence.[10]

But his lenience is shown also in other matters of law, even when the ritual practice is not really the consideration. His guiding principle is his love for his fellow man. Commenting on the text *In righteousness shalt thou judge thy neighbour* (Lev. 19:15), after giving the simple meaning of the Hebrew word *tsedek*, righteousness, Rashi offers the talmudic teaching that the Bible here instructs us to give our fellow man the full benefit of the doubt and to be as liberal towards him as charity would allow.

Many of the questions addressed to him dealt with the problems arising out of the use by Jews of Gentile wine. The law prohibits Jews from using such wine on the premise that it could have been used for pagan religious purposes. Rashi shows himself more accommodating to the realities of the economic situation where many Jews as well as Gentiles in that part of France were vine growers. He argues that the Christians were not pagans and that therefore there is no fear that their wine, or wine handled by Christians, could have been used for idolatrous purposes. While prohibiting the drinking of Gentile wine, Rashi nevertheless allowed Jews to derive other benefits from it. In another Responsum Rashi supports his lenient attitude to the question on the argument that the Gentiles in his day are actually quite ignorant of the pagan practices of primitive ages. He wrote, 'Gentiles nowadays are not familiar with the intricacies of idol worship and they are therefore to be considered like new-born infants whose touch cannot make the wine forbidden to Jews.' He seems to be reporting from personal knowledge when he says, 'We have neither heard nor seen any one of them [Gentiles] pouring out wine for idol worship.'[11]

Another Responsum touches on Rashi's views on trade with the Gentiles. The Talmud prohibits cattle dealing with non-Jews.[12] No doubt this early prohibition was also based on the suspicion that such trade could involve the Jew in facilitating idolatrous or pagan practices. Rashi remarked, however, that when the Talmud promulgated such a law the Jews lived all together and it was easier for them to do trade with each other, '... but at present, when we are a minority in the midst of our neighbours we cannot conform to so disastrous a measure.'[13]

Above all, Rashi was a man of peace who tried to instil the virtues of harmony and goodwill into communal relationships. He believed that communal peace was an effective defence against the pain inflicted upon the Jews by their enemies. He wrote, 'Apply yourself to the cultivation of peace. See how your neighbours are troubled by the greatest evil and how the Christians delight in them. Harmony will be your defence against envy and prevent it from dominating you.'[14]

This same love of peace is exhibited in his comment on the generation of the Tower of Babel. Rashi asks the question, Who were the bigger sinners, the generation of the great Flood or the generation of the Tower of Babel? The former did not rebel against God Himself, whereas the latter actually rebelled against God and attempted to supplant His sovereignty. Yet the people at the time of the Flood were all destroyed and the generation of the Tower was not destroyed but simply dispersed. Why the difference? Rashi answers that the people at the time of the Flood robbed one another and created social chaos, while the generation of the Tower dealt with each other in a spirit of brotherly love and unity, as Scripture testifies—*And the whole earth was of one language and of one speech* (Gen. 11:1). This proves, says Rashi, that controversy is hateful to God while peace is beloved.[15]

In the chapter of Rebuke (Lev. 26) the Bible lists all the material blessings which Israel will enjoy as a reward for obedience to God's law. Then in a new verse the Bible promises the blessing of peace. Whereon Rashi remarks, 'From this we can learn that peace is the equivalent of all other blessings put together.'[16]

In line with his advocacy of the virtue of peace in the community, Rashi always tried to strengthen peaceful domestic relationships between husband and wife, parents and children.

Like Aaron, the first High Priest, and the first-century sage Hillel, Rashi was one who pursued peace. His correspondence gives evidence of his passion for fostering this virtue, and he could even write scathingly of anyone guilty of breaking up family unity.

In spite of his generally liberal attitude, Rashi was a strict upholder of traditional practice and was himself extremely pious in every detail of the law. In case of doubt he recognized the stricter interpretation as an alternative for some people and remarked, 'Blessed be he who does this,' but at the same time he allowed for the more lenient interpretation. He could adopt the stricter ruling for himself without demanding that it be the norm for others.

Rashi himself did not collect his Responsa (such deliberate collection by their authors was not known until much later), but his disciples did succeed in gathering together at least part of their master's correspondence. From the collection available to us we learn a great deal about the social conditions of the time, and about Rashi's decisions in matters of law. Even more relevant to our theme in this chapter, we obtain a clearer picture of the man, with his warm personality, kindly, considerate, humble, lenient and above all the man who espoused the value of peace.

If Rashi had left us nothing but the record of a pious, compassionate and scholarly personality, it would have been sufficient for his memory to be honoured. But of course he left us a great deal more in his monumental commentaries on the Bible and Talmud, the two great works which make him one of the most outstanding masters of Jewish thought.

3

THE BIBLE COMMENTARY

I

Bible interpretation is as old as the earliest organized religious community in ancient Israel. The first teachers of the sacred Law were the priests, and the evidence of the prophet Malachi is to the point: *For the priest's lips should keep knowledge, and they [the people] should seek the Law at his mouth; for he is the messenger of the Lord of hosts* (2:27). In the period of the return of the Jews from Babylonian exile, in the fifth century BCE, Ezra the scribe, the priests and the levites were the readers and the interpreters as they assembled the people around their platforms in the public places and instructed them in the Law. Thus the Bible describes the scene, *And they caused the people to understand the Law ... And they read in the book, in the Law of God, distinctly; and they gave the sense, and called them to understand the reading* (Neh. 8:7–8).

With the close of the biblical canon, the rabbis undertook the interpretation of the Bible with detailed care. Leading rabbinic authorities identified principles by which the literal text of the Bible could be interpreted and its meaning extended. So Hillel (first century CE) had a system of seven such rules,[1] a century later Rabbi Ishmael popularized a list of thirteen principles,[2] while Rabbi Eliezer ben Yose built a system of as many as thirty-two hermeneutic principles.[3]

As a result of all this interpretation the literal meaning of the text was extended to yield many additional teachings, some of them important legal points, others dealing with ethical and other religious issues. The rabbinic interpretation could even depart from the traditional text and suggest an alternative reading whenever a special lesson was intended. A good example of this homiletic method can be noted. On the verse *All thy children shall be taught of the Lord; and great shall be the peace of thy children* (Isa. 54:13), the rabbis make a play on the Hebrew word *banim*, 'children', and read *bonim*, 'builders', offering the homily, 'Call them not thy children but thy builders.'[4] Clearly, the rabbis of the time knew the correct reading of the verse, but they wanted to preach a nice sermon on the vital importance of Jewish education; for the children will grow up to become the future builders of the community.

In the period of the Talmud the practice of translating the Torah into the vernacular, during the public reading of the Law on sabbaths and festivals, was widespread. The translations were frequently accompanied by interpretations, which often ran the risk of going beyond the meaning of the text. In the hands of expert exegetes this could be controlled, but the interpreters sometimes introduced an ambiguous element, so the rabbis warned that no verse can be explained in a way that upsets its plain meaning.[5] They accepted that there was a primary meaning to the text and that this was its plain meaning; all other interpretations are secondary, and they can be advanced to teach additional lessons only so long as these secondary interpretations and their derived lessons do not contradict the plain meaning. In this way the plain meaning takes on a place of first importance in the Bible text. But the Bible is also a storehouse of implied and secondary meanings for which the text is seen as a valuable vehicle. In time these took on a life and importance of their own, so that, while the rabbis never questioned the plain meaning as of first importance, they insisted that the literal interpretation of the Scriptures is only one of several different ways in which the reader is challenged to understand the sacred text. In typical rabbinic hyperbole they stated that the Torah can be understood in seventy different ways, and they noted in support of this the verse *Is not My word like as fire, saith the Lord ... and like a hammer which breaks the rock in pieces* (Jer. 23:29).

A popular mnemonic indicates the four principal ways in which the Bible can be interpreted and understood. The mnemonic is the Hebrew word *pardes*, 'orchard', which is spelled with the four Hebrew letters PRDS: *peshat* (P), the plain meaning, *remez* (R), an allusion to another teaching altogether, *derush* (D), the homiletic and usually the ethical teaching to be discovered in the text, and *sod* (S), indicating the mystical lesson hidden in the text. Let us look at an example which clearly illustrates this four-fold method of interpretation. The verse chosen is Genesis 18:5. The context is the story of the visit by three unknown persons, or angels, to the patriarch Abraham as he is seated at the door of his tent during the heat of the day. Abraham does not know who they are and he sees them as passing travellers weary from their journey in the desert heat. He welcomes the strangers most warmly and urges them to accept the shelter and hospitality of his tent. In his invitation to rest and refresh themselves he says, *And I will fetch a morsel of bread, and stay ye your hearts*... Here is a brief account of the four kinds of interpretation based on this text.

1. *Peshat.* The plain meaning is obvious. Abraham offers simple basic refreshments to his three guests.

2. *Remez.* The allusion. While a guest may be invited to lead in the Grace after Meals, it is appropriate for the master of the house himself to recite the blessing over the bread before the meal. The phrase *And I will fetch a morsel of bread* points to the proper procedure to be followed by a host.

3. *Derush.* The homily. There are several accepted lessons here. One is particularly good. Abraham promises only *a morsel of bread*, but he proceeds to prepare a veritable banquet for his guests (vv. 6–8). Good people try to do more than they promise.

4. *Sod.* The mystical meaning. In this method the actual words of the text are the external cover for an inner and deeper meaning. This mystical meaning was much beloved by Kabbalists and mystics in a later period in Jewish history, but it is represented in talmudic Judaism as well. According to this, Abraham's promise of bread really refers to Torah teaching which is like the staff of life, and the refreshment is thus purely spiritual.

In a sense this four-fold method legitimized all non-literal interpretations of the Scriptures and the widespread use of the methods of allusion, homily and mysticism ensued. So long as they did not upset the primary place of *peshat*, the plain meaning, no harm was done—quite the contrary, because in fact the text was greatly enriched by countless new and often profound lessons uncovered by this many-sided interpretation. In practice, methods 2, 3 and 4 came to be known conveniently under the single term *derush* and it is this term which we shall henceforth use throughout this examination to denote all non-literal interpretations of the Bible text. The vast corpus of rabbinic literature known as Midrash is the exploration of these non-literal methods of interpretation.

The word Midrash comes from the Hebrew *darash* to expound or to enquire. The Midrash is a series of works written over a period of nearly a thousand years and compiled in different countries. It offers an exposition of the biblical books, sometimes of nearly every verse in a chapter. Although some midrashic works concentrate on the legalistic aspects of Judaism, most of them are distinctly non-legalistic and are what is termed *aggadah*. This term is fairly comprehensive. It includes the legends of the Jews, which are often elaborations of the biblical story, a great deal of folklore, dealing with angels, demons, the netherworld, the after-life and other matters supernatural, and a great deal of moral philosophy, which it frequently teaches through fable, anecdote, parable or extended story. Finally, the *aggadah* submits teachings on rabbinic theology which it derives from the comments on the text of the Bible. The meanings of these central terms, Midrash and *aggadah*, are significant because, as we shall see, Rashi uses these sources very extensively. Because the method of *derush* was used very widely, and particularly because of its great popularity with the people, the rabbis were at times constrained to remind their readers—and themselves—of the primary place which they insisted should be retained by the *peshat*.

It is relevant, within this context, to point out that the Christian Church from its earliest times employed non-literal and especially mystical explanations of the Bible text, particularly of the Prophets and the Psalms, in order to discern allusions to the Christian Messiah. Their interpretative exercises were known to Rashi, who attempts to deal with them in his commentaries.[6] He was aware of Jerome's (fourth century) interpretation of the 'suffering servant of the Lord' in the prophecy of Isaiah as reference to the suffering Jesus, and counters this with his own interpretation closer to the *peshat*. Incidentally, it is not likely that Rashi read Jerome in the original Latin, but it is thought that his grandson Samuel knew enough Latin to acquaint Rashi with the Christian interpretations. In any case, Rashi lived in close enough proximity to the Christians who could have given him at least second-hand knowledge of Jerome. Although he himself engaged in some gentle polemic in his commentaries, he warned his disciples against engaging in discussion with the *minim* or *mesitim*, identified variously as Christians, heretics and sectarians.

Two movements in medieval Jewish history and biblical interpretation helped to keep a proper balance between *peshat* and *derush*, and even to elevate the primary place of *peshat*. The first was the work of the masoretes, the scholars of the *Masorah*. The word *Masorah* means 'tradition' and in our context it refers to the transmission of the traditional text of the Bible. During the many centuries before printing, their work was especially important to make sure that errors did not creep into the numerous hand-written copics of books of the Bible. The early scribes, who were called *soferim*, even counted the letters of the Pentateuch to make sure that there were no additions or omissions in the holy text.[7] Some of the most distinguished rabbis were *soferim*; the most famous of them was Rabbi Meir (second century). The motivation was clear enough—to emphasize the unalterable text of the Bible. The Jewish insistence that the text was inviolable necessarily had some effect on the interpretative approach of the scholar to the sacred text. The Talmud also contains numerous rulings about the order of the books, the divisions into sections, as well as laws about the actual manner of the writing, the permitted kinds of parchment and special points about unique calligraphy for certain letters and phrases. In addition to all this written regulation, which was codified in the Talmud,[8] there was a considerable oral tradition, particularly in connection with verse divisions in the Bible; at the beginning there was no separation in writing between the verses—just as even to this day there is no full stop in the text of the sacred scrolls of the Torah and other scrolls. Other traditions which were orally handed down related to the accentuation of the Hebrew words and to the method of the intonation of the Scriptures during public reading.

The great step in the transmission of all the *Masorah*, including all the oral traditions, the accents, the vowel and punctuation signs and the permitted variant readings of a word (a word to be read in a way different to the manner in which it was spelled), was achieved in the period following the seventh century when the masoretes wrote down the entire corpus of the traditional text together with their masoretic notes, which were placed at the side of the page. All this, together with important strides in the field of grammar, made the exact meaning of the Hebrew text of the Bible more or less definitive. With such an exact Bible text the scene was set also for a greater insistence on accurate interpretation, with the *peshat* recognized as primary.

The second great help in the pursuit of the literal meaning of the text came as a result of the Karaite schism. This movement began in Babylon during the second half of the eighth century as a result of a fierce dispute over the leadership of the community. The Karaites, as the Hebrew name implies, were believers in the literal word of the Law and rejected the talmudic and rabbinic interpretations of the Scriptures. Since their credo was based on the acceptance of the written word, it necessarily followed that a close study of the Scriptures became their chief occupation. The arguments between the Rabbanites and the Karaites raged in great intensity over a period of nearly two hundred years. It caused divisiveness and hatred and the results of the schism were socially destructive. Nevertheless, one important positive result did ensue from the controversy and that was, as we have suggested, the more determined study of the Bible text. The leader of the Karaites, Anan ben David, declared that everything is in the Bible, so that it is not necessary to go to the Talmud and the rabbis for any further explanation. He exhorted, 'Study and search the Bible, for you will find everything in it.' The most outstanding leader of the Rabbanite side was Saadiah Gaon (882–942). He is chiefly known as the first of a long line of systematic philosophers of Judaism, but not less important in his career was the way he defended the rabbinic position against the

Karaites. To do this the more effectively, the philosopher also concentrated his brilliant mind on the questions of biblical interpretation. He translated the Bible into Arabic—the language most spoken by the Jews of his day. Secondly, he wrote a partial commentary on the Bible which rests chiefly on the *peshat*. All Saadiah's previous work in the field of Hebrew grammar led to his work on the Bible translation and interpretation. His translation is not a literal one, since he intended it to be more popular and easily read by the average layman. His commentary, called *Tafsir*, is rational and avoids dependence on too much *derush*. The great medieval grammarian Menahem ibn Saruk speaks of Saadiah's accuracy of interpretation and of his comprehensive grasp of linguistics.

We can now proceed to consider more specifically the massive contribution of Rashi's commentary and the unique place it holds in biblical and rabbinic literature. We will begin with a general statement of Rashi's aim; then say something about his style and about his skill as a translator-interpreter. This will be followed by some comments on his grammar. Finally, we will examine the most important aspect of his commentary—the place of *peshat* and *derush*, concluding with a number of examples illustrating the Rashi method.

II

Rashi worked on his Bible and Talmud commentaries at the same time and over many years. Using his notes as guides in his teaching, he had the raw material on which he laboured to produce a complete and systematic work and, careful and responsible as he was as a teacher, he was especially so as an author, taking great pains to correct and revise his work all the time. A Rabbi Isaac of Vienna, who was in possession of an autographed manuscript of Rashi's commentary on the Bible, described it as surrounded on many pages by numerous revisions, deletions and other corrections.[9]

Unlike his commentary on the Talmud, Rashi wrote his work on the Bible in the order in which the books appear in the canon. The commentaries on the books of Chronicles, the last books in the Hebrew Bible, are not his, since he died before he could complete his writing on the entire Scriptures.[10]

In approaching an examination of his Bible commentaries, we have to know what it was that Rashi tried to achieve. Perhaps it would be easier first of all to say what he did not try to accomplish. He did not examine and explain a complete subject or a law according to any philosophical system or theological concepts (he was no Maimonides). Consequently we will not find in Rashi any profound explanation of a biblical teaching. He will not tell us anything about Jewish religious philosophy, or present his views on any of the theological concepts which are central to the Jewish faith. It is therefore vain to look into Rashi for an exposition of even such basic teachings as the Creation, Free Will, Divine Revelation, the nature of the soul, the after-life, or even about the concept of God in Judaism. Of course it is not too difficult to get an impression of Rashi's beliefs on all these pillars of Jewish philosophy, but he does not deal with any of them separately as subjects to be studied for their own importance. It is not even likely that Rashi would have felt that he was knowledgeable enough to expound on those subjects. Although the philosophical works of Saadiah Gaon were written about a hundred years before Rashi, there is no evidence that the Master of Troyes was aware of them. Judah Halevi lived not very long after Rashi's time, but he was thirty-five years younger and nothing he wrote would have reached Rashi. Maimonides, the most significant Jewish philosopher-theologian, was born thirty years after Rashi's death. Between Halevi and Maimonides there was no one whose philosophical writings could have been brought to Rashi's attention. In any case, Saadiah wrote in Egypt, Halevi and other major Jewish philosophers of the Rashi period in Spain. Legend apart, there is no evidence that Rashi had any contact with his peers in Spain, and he thus remained uninfluenced by the philosophical trends prevalent in that country.

But over and above all this, Rashi's first aim was entirely different: he wished to explain not concepts, but the meaning of words and phrases, as well as other difficulties that may be found in the text itself. This purpose is abundantly clear in his Talmud commentary where, without Rashi's explanation of the difficult text, the average student could not have gone very far, but it applies also to his Bible commentary. Here too, his guiding hand is always present to give the meaning of a difficult word or phrase, to reconcile conflicts in the text or to anticipate questions relating to it. In the course of his examination and explanation of the text, Rashi introduces us to the fascinating world of rabbinic literature when he gives a rabbinic legend, homily or exposition, especially when the plain meaning of the text seems to him to be inadequate and when he believes that a rabbinic homily can cast some light on our understandng of the text itself. This particular method of interpretation is central to Rashi's Bible commentary—indeed, it is the unique feature of his work on the Bible and we will deal with it separately. Meanwhile, let us survey some of the other features of Rashi's Bible commentary.

Rashi's skill as a teacher and commentator is immediately apparent in two vital matters: he is clear and he is concise, two qualities which often go together; but not always. There are some teachers and commentators who, in their efforts at clarity, become verbose and stuff their writings with repetitious explanations and unnecessary detail. It is said of Rashi's grandson, Samuel ben Meir, that he showed some commentaries that he had written on the Talmud to his grandfather, and Rashi teased him about the length of the work, saying, 'If you were to explain the whole of the Talmud in this fashion you would find your commentary so heavy that you would need a carriage to carry it!' On the other hand, Abraham ibn Ezra, the twelfth-century Spanish Bible commentator, is often concise; yet his work is so obscure at times that even scholars are at a loss to discover his meaning. By contrast, Rashi is the exemplar of a commentator with such clarity of expression and explanation that no one need be in doubt as to what he is saying. Further, his comments, with relatively few exceptions, are written with a remarkable economy of language, so that there is rarely a phrase or even a word which is superfluous or missing. Students of Rashi's commentary have been known to tell anecdotes of having been challenged by their teachers to rewrite a piece of Rashi, saying the same thing as the Master but omitting a word or two: they found the task impossible. Similarly, they would fail to make Rashi's explanation any clearer by their addition of a word or words. Rashi's literary style is exemplary. The clarity of his comments and the conciseness of his language are among the most outstanding features of his commentary.

Next to questions of method and style, the significant characteristic of Rashi's *peshat* is his search for accurate meaning, and his attempt to make sense of difficult words and phrases. He frequently resorts to simple explanations of his own by giving an alternative Hebrew word where he thought that the biblical word might not be understood. Thus, the Hebrew word *hishiani* (Gen. 3:13), translated 'beguiled me', is very rare. He therefore offers another word which is easily understood, *hitiani*. Again, *vayisha* (ibid., 4:4) is translated by *vayifen*, 'and He had regard', and *berachah* (ibid., 33:11) is translated with *minha*, 'a gift'. In Leviticus 19:2 Rashi shows himself a translator *par excellence*. The text is *Ye shall be holy*, Hebrew *kedoshim*. But what is the true meaning of *kadosh*, 'holy'? Rashi's translation is *perushim*, i.e. 'separated from immorality': his skill as a translator helps us to take note also of the real meaning of holiness.

In the same vein, we notice the way Rashi treats synonyms or near-synonyms in the Bible. Hebrew does not easily tolerate such words and Rashi knows that each separate word is unlike any other and has a meaning of its own.[11] A mere handful of examples of Rashi's constant concern to pinpoint with absolute accuracy the meaning of similar words can be seen in his explanation of *mezuzoth*, 'side-posts' and *mashkof*, 'lintel' (Ex. 12:7); *petza*, 'a bloody wound' and *haburah*, 'a wound with internal bleeding' (ibid., 21:25); *shallal*, 'booty of clothing and ornaments' and *malkoah*, 'human prey or livestock' (Num. 31:11); *etzadah*, 'jewels on the legs' and *tzamid*, 'jewels on the hand' (verse 50); *pahad*, 'fear on those who are near' and *morah*, 'dread on those who are far off' (Deut. 11:25).

Rashi's extraordinary philological skills were sharpened by his personal knowledge of many everyday occupations. He was familiar with agricultural work, he knew what went on in the

market place and he had a good knowledge of the manu-
facturer's work in many trades. His commentaries on the
chapters describing the making of the tabernacle and its holy
furniture are filled with interesting details which indicate a wide
knowledge of technical and worldly matters. He knows
something of metalwork, coin stamping, working with silk and
wood, weaving and baking. It is known that in several places
Rashi even drew illustrations to show his readers the shape or
plan of an object. Unfortunately, these illustrations were
dropped from the printed editions and were subsequently lost.

In accordance with his aim of making the text clearly
understood, Rashi relies very frequently on the Aramaic
translation of Onkelos. Popularly known as the Targum, 'the
translation', this second-century translation of the Pentateuch
was highly esteemed by the rabbis. Rashi frequently finds
support for his *peshat* by pointing to the literal meaning given in
the rendering of Onkelos.

Rashi often resorts also to translation of words into the
vernacular. The Jews of France spoke French and Rashi wants
his readers and students to understand the biblical word. What is
more natural for a good teacher than to offer them a direct
translation into the language with which they are familiar? Such
an explanation is introduced with the word *b'laaz*, which is
explained as a mnemonic standing for *b'lashon am zar*, i.e. 'in a
foreign language'.[12] The plural of this mnemonic is variously
given as *loazim* or *leazim*; more accurately *laazim*. In the Bible
commentary there are about a thousand such *laazim*, with about
two hundred and fifty in the Pentateuch alone. The Talmud
commentary contains more than twice as many. The entire
collection of over three thousand such words is a veritable
treasure for researchers into medieval French as spoken in the
north of the country. Since Hebrew is such a phonetic language,
the French word as transcribed in the Hebrew letters also offers a
good guide to the pronunciation. The word list of Rashi's
medieval French is all the more valuable because many of the
words deal with ordinary items which were in everyday use. It is
noteworthy that Rashi employs the *laazim* extensively in his
commentary on the chapters dealing with the construction of

the tabernacle and its furniture, in his treatment of the sections on the clean and unclean animals, beasts, birds and fowl, and in his description of the categories of diseases found in the Bible. Not many definitive studies have been made on this aspect of Rashi's writings, probably because it is too specialist a subject, but the few studies which do exist are of great importance in the study of Old French.[13] In line with Rashi's intent, some late editions of Rashi's commentary translated the French *laazim*, which Yiddish-speaking Jews could not understand, into equivalent German-Yiddish words.

Since Rashi was chiefly set on giving the plain meaning of the text, it was natural that he should investigate the grammar of the Hebrew word or phrase. As a result, his commentary contains numerous notes that provide a most valuable early contribution to the grammar of the Hebrew language. A modern grammarian may find Rashi's observations and even his terms a little strange. This is only natural since the scientific study of the Hebrew language was still in its infancy. Yet, although they were rudimentary, Rashi's notes on grammar were still advanced for their time. Rashi had predecessors in the field. Two of them were Menahem ibn Saruk and Dunash ben Labrat, both of whom lived about a hundred years earlier, Menahem in Spain and Dunash in Fez. Rashi was familiar with their writing and frequently refers to them in his commentaries: he also disagrees with them at times, particularly in his theory of the triliteral root of weak verbs. There were other grammarians who wrote in Arabic, such as Judah Hayyuj and ibn Janah, but the Hebrew translation of their works did not appear until long after Rashi's death, and it is hardly likely that Rashi would have known about their original writings.

Rashi is particularly skilful in explaining the various Hebrew prepositions to suit the context in which they occur. The dative *el*, the accusative *eth* and the ablative *b'* are not always treated literally to mean 'to', 'it' or 'in'. Rashi often suggests that we have to understand them in entirely different ways in order to give better meaning to the phrases in which they occur. He thus provides a new and extended usage for the Hebrew preposition.[14] He treats the Hebrew conjunction and prefix in the same free way. Thus the Hebrew conjunction *vav* is not a simple conjunction: it can mean 'or' and sometimes it introduces a conditional clause.[15] In the same way the Hebrew word *ki* can carry one of several possible meanings such as 'when', 'if', 'because', 'perhaps' and 'although',[16] depending on the context and therefore what makes the best sense.

Reference has already been made to Rashi's disagreement with Menahem and Dunash on the triliteral root of the weak verb. He also commented on the verb tenses and showed how a verb in a continuous tense will sometimes be expressed in the future and sometimes in the present tense.[17]

Even the Hebrew accents are important to Rashi in his search for accurate meaning. By Rashi's time the *teamim*, or accent signs, and cantillation marks had already been developed into a full system of punctuation of the sacred text.[18] The *teamim* were more than signs to indicate the cantillation of a word. They served as grammatical aids to the correct reading of the word and also as a help to its correct meaning. An accent sign can give the correct tense of a verb and so Rashi paid very close attention to these signs.[19]

Finally, Rashi accepts with little question that the order of words in a sentence can be misleading; to make better sense the words may have to be transposed. The rabbis in the Talmud had already discussed this question and some of them are shown to be in favour of transposition. A well-known example of this is found in I Samuel 3:3, where the text has *And the lamp of God was not gone out, and Samuel was laid down to sleep in the temple of the Lord, where the ark of God was*... The Talmud discusses the difficulty of the text, which seems to suggest that Samuel went to sleep in the sacred precincts, i.e. *where the ark of God was*. The solution offered is that the phrase *and Samuel was laid down to sleep* should be transferred to the end of the sentence. Thus the difficulty is removed. Another and even more obvious need for transposition is found in Genesis 41:57, where the order of the Hebrew words in that verse would produce the translation *And all the countries came into Egypt to buy corn to Joseph*. Obviously *to buy corn* and *to Joseph* should be transposed. Rashi rightly notes this. The interesting thing here is that he does not say that the sacred text is in any way defective or that it should be rearranged: he simply offers the correct meaning based on the transposition. However, in other places where Rashi adopts the same method of interpretation he explicitly states that the word order has to be rearranged before arriving at the correct meaning of the text.[20] His failure to say so as explicitly in every such instance gives the impression that the pious scholar is disinclined to arrive at his interpretations through emending even the order of the words. For Rashi, as for all scholars of his time, the text is sacred; it is Divine, and therefore it is not subject to alteration.

As we have indicated, Rashi is of course interested in very much more than just explaining the meaning of words and phrases. He is, in addition, the expounder of the sense of the text. Through his commentary he is at pains to give his readers the lessons, the teachings, the laws and above all their meanings. To this end he is sometimes constrained to reconcile apparent contradictions in two biblical verses. Thus, Exodus 12:15 rules *Seven days shall ye eat unleavened bread*, while in Deuteronomy 16:8 the law states, *Six days shall ye eat unleavened bread*. The obvious contradiction is reconciled by Rashi, in accord with rabbinic exegesis: the two verses together teach us that the eating of unleavened bread is obligatory only on the first day of the Passover Festival. For the other six days, there remains only the prohibition against eating leavened bread.

Another apparent contradiction is noted by Rashi in Exodus 19:20 and 20:19. The first of these two verses records, *And the Lord came down upon Mount Sinai* while the second one states in God's name, *Ye yourselves have seen that I have talked with you from heaven*. Did God speak to Israel from Sinai or from heaven? In such a case, Rashi reminds us, we need a third verse which will reconcile the other two. This is found in Deuteronomy 4:36, where it says, *Out of the heaven He made thee hear His voice ... and upon earth He made thee see His great fire*. This is classical rabbinic exegesis. At the same time he also reminds us of the Midrash, which poetically describes God as joining heaven to earth to provide the scene for His Divine revelation.

One more example will suffice under this heading. The visit of the strangers to Lot (Gen. 19:1) is introduced as follows: *And the two angels came unto Sodom at even; and Lot sat in the gate of Sodom.* However, when they visit Abraham (*ibid.*, 18:2) they are referred to not as angels but as men. The small point does not escape the gimlet eye of Rashi, who submits that in Abraham's case they appear to him like men since Abraham himself was a man of sublime spiritual nature. Lot, being so unused to such manifestations, would more easily have thought of them as angels.

III

We must now consider the central feature of Rashi's commentary, his use of *peshat* and *derush*.

Rashi's aim was to explain the Bible text according to its *peshat*. He was probably convinced that such a method was especially called for in his time to counterbalance the main direction of rabbinic interpretation which was midrashic.[21] Thus, in many places in his commentary, he insists that his aim is to explain the simple meaning of the text. Take Genesis 33:20 as an example. The text is, *And he erected there an altar and called it El-elohe Israel.* Rashi records the rabbinic *derush* that God called Jacob *el*, a god. But he rejects this and says, 'My job is to explain the *peshat*', and he does so by saying that Jacob gave the altar a name which commemorated the fact that miracles were wrought for him by Israel's, i.e. Jacob's, God.

In the same context, let us look at Genesis 4:8. *And Cain spoke unto Abel his brother. And it came to pass when they were in the field, that Cain rose up against Abel his brother and slew him.* The first phrase in the sentence seems defective since there is no mention of what Cain said to Abel. As can be imagined, rabbinic legend rushes in to fill the gap of the unrecorded conversation. Rashi notes that; but he will have none of it in that context. Instead, he offers a simple explanation: 'Cain quarrelled with Abel and found a pretext to kill him. That is the plain and correct meaning.'

Of particular interest is Rashi's comment on Genesis 3:8. The

Bible text records, *And they heard the voice of the Lord God walking in the garden towards the cool of the day*. Rashi reminds us that there are many rabbinic legends relating to the attempt of Adam and Eve to escape God's attention after their sin. But he insists that his aim is not to purvey *derush* but to explain the plain meaning. His statement here is worth quoting in full. 'There are many pieces of aggadic midrash on this verse which the rabbis have told in Bereshith Rabbah and in other midrashim. But my simple task is to concentrate on the plain meaning of the verses and to introduce *aggadah* only when it can really help to give sense to the text.'

This last point is worth following. Rashi's commentary includes a very great amount of *derush*, but claims to introduce rabbinic legend only when it can help us to understand the meaning of the text. The words of the Bible might be difficult as written; there may be a problem with the grammar or even with the teaching the verse is to convey. At all events, there is a question which has to be solved. If it can be solved by the method of *peshat*, well and good: this is exactly what Rashi sets out to achieve. However, it sometimes happens that the *peshat* solution falls short for one reason or another, in which case Rashi will illuminate the text with an item of rabbinic folklore or midrash which brings a new dimension to the interpretation and helps frequently to a clearer understanding. This is often his way with his use of *derush* and his Bible commentary is replete with examples of the method. In these cases, it is not *derush* for the sake of telling a good story, but primarily to explain the text. Rashi's folkloristic explanations abound with examples of this kind, and it is significant that the commentator knows exactly why he introduces the *derush*. Thus, he adds an aggadic touch to the story of the birth of Jacob and Esau (Gen. 25:26) by first saying, 'I heard an aggadic midrash which explains the verse according to its plain meaning.' Or again, in his explanation of the verse in Jacob's blessing of Joseph, Rashi notes that there are many rabbinic legends, but that the one he has chosen is the best because, 'it tends to explain the verse' (Gen. 49:22).

As an extension of his method, Rashi will sometimes say that the verse cannot really be satisfactorily explained by the *peshat* and the verse seems to call out for an explanation by *derush*. Thus on Genesis 1:1, the grammatical problem of the very first word leads Rashi to exclaim, 'This verse really asks to be expounded midrashically.' Similarly with Genesis 1:4, where Rashi insists, 'Here we really need an aggadic explanation.' The prenatal struggle of Jacob and Esau (Gen. 25:22) evokes Rashi's exclamation, 'Whether you like it or not, this verse must be treated aggadically.'

That the *derush* brings with it an additional and useful lesson most certainly encourages Rashi to recall the legend, but that is really of secondary importance to his main task. Take, for example, Genesis 24:67. *And Isaac brought her [Rebekah] into his mother Sarah's tent, and took Rebekah, and she became his wife; and he loved her.* Of course, in English the meaning is fairly straightforward, but the Hebrew text really says something else: *Vayevieha Yitzhak ha-ohelah Sarah imo.* Now the word *ha-ohelah* cannot be a noun in the dative with a construct form, so the translation 'to the tent *of* Sarah his mother' is inaccurate. The Hebrew words should be translated simply, 'to the tent: Sarah his mother' and there is no construct form here. In order to provide a meaning which is closer to the Hebrew text, Rashi actually translates the phrase, 'And Isaac brought her into the tent. And she was like his mother Sarah, in her piety and in her charitable conduct.' As usual with this method, Rashi is not original: he simply transmits the rabbinic *derush* in his own way, but his purpose in doing so is perfectly clear. It is to explain the actual text and to solve the problem of the difficult grammatical structure of the Hebrew word *ha-ohelah*. That his *derush* offers a lovely homily in the importance of generational values is merely an added bonus.

Let us follow one or two more examples in the Isaac story which also illustrate Rashi's method of expanding his explanation into *derush* when clarification of *peshat* demands it. *And Isaac entreated the Lord for his wife because she was barren* (Gen. 25:21). This is the acceptable translation and meaning. But the Hebrew preposition *le-nochah* calls for a different and even more accurate translation. The Hebrew word really means 'opposite' rather than 'for'. This allows Rashi to introduce the rabbinic picture of

Isaac praying in one corner of the tent and Rebekah praying in the opposite corner—each petitioning God. The *derush*, of course, might be a little sermonette with a variety of different lessons, yet Rashi's motive in bringing it to his readers' attention is because that *derush* actually fits in better with the *peshat*.

One more illustration from the same story. *And when her [Rebekah's] days to be delivered were fulfilled, behold there were twins in her womb* (Gen. 25:24). The translation is simple *peshat*. But it has to be noted that the Hebrew word for 'twins', *te-omim*, is spelled defectively, as if it were written *teomm*. On this, Rashi remarks that the spelling is defective in this word since the twinship of Jacob and Esau was defective. One was righteous and the other was wicked.

Finally, and to emphasize the same point, in many instances where Rashi finds that the *derush* is really unnecessary then he will first point out the existence of the *aggadah*, but will then go on to say that, since he is more interested in *peshat*, he will omit the *derush*. In Genesis 3:8—the story of Adam and Eve in the garden of Eden—Rashi notes, 'There are many midrashim which the rabbis have written down... but since my task is only to explain the simple meaning of the text, I will introduce *aggadah* only when it reconciles the words with the context.'

Some emphasis has been placed on this aspect of Rashi's Bible commentary—his primary intention of giving the *peshat*, introducing *derush* chiefly in order to throw light on the plain meaning—for two reasons. First, it helps us to an understanding of his method; secondly, his liberal use of *derush* was misunderstood, and therefore unfairly criticized, in some quarters.

Abraham ibn Ezra, the twelfth-century Spanish grammarian, philosopher and Bible exegete also wrote a commentary on the Bible—very different from that of Rashi. Where ibn Ezra was not prejudiced by his philosophical opinions he tried to follow the strict *peshat*. Perhaps on account of this, as well as his rather restless nature and scientific bent, he saw Rashi's use of *derush* as excessive and unscientific: 'The Talmud has declared that the *peshat* must never lose its rights, but the following generations gave the first place to *derush*, as Rashi did, who pursued this method in his commentary on the entire Bible though he believed he was using *peshat*. In his work there is not one rational explanation out of a thousand.'[22] Those are indeed harsh words, but if that criticism seems severe it is relatively mild compared with a work written by one Abraham ibn Daud in thirteenth-century Spain. It is so critical of Rashi that the copyist was moved to cross out several passages of the most extreme part of the criticism: he also warns against its indiscriminate distribution.[23]

Some of the criticism can be justified, particularly with regard to Rashi's obvious fondness for a homily. He is a warm-hearted man of the people, and it is clear that he loved *derush* even when he insisted that his real aim was to give the *peshat*. He knew his readers and he understood, quite rightly, that for many of them the *aggadah* was more attractive than the dry *peshat*. His natural feeling for *derush* proved to his readers that the Bible record was a warm and intensely human document, and in the course of time the masses of the people who read Rashi embraced his commentaries all the more enthusiastically precisely because of the prominence of *derush*. Rashi attempted, as we have seen, to limit its use to the areas where it would have a direct relevance to the *peshat*, but from time to time he may have forgotten this limitation and allowed his love for *derush* to take the ascendancy. This happens: not very often, but it does happen. Take, for example, Genesis 1:26: *And God said: 'Let us make man in our image after our likeness and let them have dominion over the fish of the sea and over the fowl of the air, and over the cattle...* The Hebrew word for *and let them have dominion* is *veyirdu*. The translation is perfectly accurate and the meaning is clear, so Rashi could easily have left it at that, but this is perhaps one of those occasions when he could not forgo a nice homily. So he suggests a *derush* which implies the alternative reading *veyerdu*, 'and they shall descend'. The lesson is a good one: if man proves worthy he will be master of all creation—and *veyirdu*, they will rule over all things. But if man proves unworthy then *veyerdu*, that is, man will sink lower than the animal world which will then have dominion over him. Here the *derush* has nothing to do with the *peshat*—on the contrary, it really interferes with it.

Another example of this kind of *derush* is interesting in its context because Rashi quotes one of his predecessors. In the curses found in Deuteronomy 27:15 ff., Rashi notes that there are eleven curses. Why not twelve, corresponding to the twelve tribes? Here Rashi tells us that he learned from Moses Ha-Darshan (the Preacher) that Moses excluded the tribe of Simeon from the list of curses because at the end of his life he blessed all the tribes of Israel except Simeon. Since he had no plan to bless Simeon he thought it fitting at least to leave that tribe out of the curses. Now the fact that Moses did not bless Simeon at the end of his leadership of Israel in the wilderness is seen in the text (Deut. 33),[24] but the correspondence of the eleven curses to the eleven tribes has no roots at all in the *peshat*. It is pure *derush*, and one can argue that it is uncharacteristic of Rashi. Nevertheless, the master commentator does from time to time, as we have admitted, take a sort of genial pleasure in the *derush* as *derush*, and many of his readers must have found his Bible commentary enriched on that account.

It would seem that Rashi himself was not unaware of the criticism of introducing too much *derush*. His famous grandson Samuel said about his grandfather's commentary: 'Our teacher, Solomon, my mother's father, has enlightened the eyes of the Dispersion, by commenting on the Bible and paying attention to the simple meaning of Scriptures. And I, Samuel, son of his son-in-law Meir of blessed memory, have often debated the issue with him. He admitted to me that if he had more time he would consider it necessary to re-write his commentaries in the light of the ordinary meaning being detected every day.'[25] In view of the fact that Rashi's first aim was to give the *peshat*, and that for the most part he succeeded in that aim, one can only conclude that, if Samuel's testimony is to be taken at its face value, towards the end of his life Rashi felt that it would have been even better had he concentrated far more on *peshat* and reduced *derush* to the absolute minimum. That he did not do so can be accepted as the good fortune of countless students of Rashi's Bible commentaries, who loved Rashi precisely because his work was not the dry explanation of *peshat* but was enlivened by the fascinating literature of rabbinic folklore. A simple comparison between the work of Rashi and that of Samuel (Rashbam) brings home this point. Rashbam's commentary on the Bible, while it is highly esteemed, is dry, and relatively unknown today except to the serious student. The comparison between the two scholars is of course an unfair one—Rashi is unique—but the point made here is that the Rashbam commentary is far more literal. Its emphasis is *peshat* and it is likely that this could at least be one important reason for its relatively limited appeal.

Another very important result of Rashi's extensive use of *derush* is his popularization of rabbinic *aggadah*. It should be remembered that in Rashi's time there were few copies of the texts. In the case of the Bible, or at least the Pentateuch, manuscripts of the sacred texts, though not abundant, were more or less sufficient to satisfy scholarly and communal needs. Even with regard to the Talmud, while full texts were extremely rare, partial texts were copied out by teachers and students for their own use. In other areas of rabbinic literature, manuscripts were even scarcer, and until the introduction of Hebrew printing some four hundred years later there were very few copies of such manuscripts. Rashi's wealth of *derush* takes in the entire range of *aggadah* from the Talmud and the Midrash: he is like a walking encyclopaedia and his memory is phenomenal. Of course he does not quote the rabbinic *aggadah* verbatim, nor does he generally give his sources; but for the average student and reader this is no real defect. The important thing is that Rashi made his readers familiar with countless rabbinic expositions which otherwise would have been unknown to them.

One further point may be made in this context. It is not only the medieval students without the written texts who were informed and enriched by Rashi's wide use of *aggadah*. In later centuries, and indeed to some extent even in our own time, there are many students who 'skip' the aggadic sections of Talmud: for them the only subject that matters is the *halachah*—the law. They thought that the folklore, homilies, stories and even philosophical-ethical teachings were not for the mature and 'serious' scholar. It seems probable that had they not learned the Bible together

with the Rashi, they would have remained largely ignorant of
the precious treasure found in rabbinic *aggadah*.

One can frequently ask why Rashi chose one particular piece of
aggadah rather than another, in cases where there was a choice.
The answer suggested here is that Rashi was very sensitive to the
ethical dimension of the *derush*. Whenever there was a good
moral lesson to be drawn from folklore Rashi was quick to
introduce it into his commentary. His *derush* is therefore not
only an aid to the understanding of the text; it is not only a
corpus of marvellous rabbinic folklore and legend; it is also a vast
storehouse of Jewish ethical teaching which impressed on
rabbinic Judaism a distinctive ethical character. Let us follow a
few examples of this aspect of Rashi's *derush*, from literally many
hundreds of texts which illustrate this feature.

Let us make man in our image (Gen. 1:26). The great teacher
comments that God consulted the angels although they did not
assist in the Creation. This teaches us the value of proper and
modest conduct, in that the leader should have enough respect
for his subordinates as to consult them.

And could not speak peaceably to him (ibid., 37:4). Joseph's
brothers could not say a kind word to him. Rashi brings out the
ethical side of this by observing that they could not be
hypocrites— thinking one thing and saying something else.

She sent to her father-in-law saying (ibid., 38:25). The context is
the story of Judah and Tamar. Rashi emphasizes the ethical
nature of Tamar's character. She would not mention him by
name so as not to put him to shame.

And they took a stone and put it under him (Ex., 17:12). Moses
sits on a hill overlooking the scene of Israel's battle with Amalek.
Rashi wonders why Moses should have to sit on a hard stone
instead of on a soft cushion. His comment is linked with the
value of involvement. Moses said, 'While Israel is in pain I
should not sit in comfort.'

He shall pay five oxen for an ox and four sheep for a sheep (ibid.,
21:37). The verse prescribes a law of restitution in a case of the
theft of these animals. Why the difference in the fine, between
stealing an ox or a sheep? Rashi brings in here two rabbinic

teachings. First, that there is less embarrassment to the thief who takes an ox and simply drives it off; so he pays more. In stealing a sheep, however, the thief already suffers some shame by being compelled to carry it; so he pays less. Secondly, one who steals an ox deprives its owner of the ox's labour, and the loss he has caused is more serious, so he has to pay more than the one who steals a sheep which has no work value for its owner.

And they were afraid to come nigh him (*ibid.*, 34:30). Moses descends from the mountain and his skin sent forth rays. Rashi brings a comment of profound psychological-ethical truth. Before they sinned with the golden calf the people were all able to experience the effulgence of the Divine radiance. But after their sin, their spiritual power was so weak that they could not even look at Moses' brilliant face.

Scarlet and hyssop (Lev. 14:4). Rashi asks, 'How shall the leper become purified?' He answers, 'He shall humble himself to become as lowly as the scarlet (literally, 'a worm') and the hyssop (the lowest plant).' Rashi's comment is an indication of the connection between physical and moral health.

Thou shalt not abhor an Egyptian, because thou wast a stranger in his land (Deut. 23:8). Although they so cruelly oppressed Israel and even drowned their male children. One can argue that Rashi does not need to explain anything here since the verse is self-explanatory. Nevertheless, he sees fit to underline the ethical dimension by saying that Israel found hospitality in Egypt during the emergency years of famine.

The value of peace is regarded as one of the highest, if not the highest, ethical value in Judaism. Rashi is not slow to emphasize this in many places in his commentary. The first place is in the story of the Tower of Babel (see Chapter 2). Here are a few other references where Rashi underlines the same ethic.

The stones of the altar had to be unhewn stones and no sword could be used to cut them (Ex. 20:22). Rashi reminds us of a rabbinic teaching that the altar of religion is made to prolong life, and therefore it may not be touched by the sword which shortens life: a relevant lesson on the ideal of peace as central to Judaism and always a timely reminder to the religious Jew where his efforts must be directed.

And I will give peace in the land (Lev. 26:6). Although the land will be adequately blessed with all material blessings. Says Rashi, 'If there is no peace then there is really nothing, because peace is the equivalent of all other blessings put together.'

And Moses sent to call Dathan and Abiram (Num. 16:12). The context is Korah's rebellion against Moses and Aaron. The two characters mentioned in our text were notorious troublemakers. Yet Moses tries hard to arbitrate and to pacify. Rashi infers that this teaches how we should always try to bring an end to communal strife, even as Moses did with Dathan and Abiram.

IV

In this section it will be useful to take a number of longer examples of Rashi's commentary on the Bible, and attempt to explain the commentary and to identify the various elements of the Rashi method which have so far been separately described. For our purpose we shall restrict ourselves to well-known parts of the Pentateuch: first, because it is easier for the general reader to follow Rashi's commentary on a text or a story which is familiar, second, the full extent of Rashi's method in *derush* is exhibited chiefly in the Five Books of Moses.

In the beginning God created the heaven and the earth (Gen. 1:1).

[RASHI] R. Isaac said: The Torah could properly have started with the passage *This month shall be unto you the beginning of months* (Ex. 12:2) because that is the first commandment given to all the people of Israel. Then why does the Torah begin with the verse, *In the beginning God created the heaven and the earth*? It is in order to emphasize the truth which is also found in the verse, *He hath declared to His people the power of His works, in giving them the heritage of the nations* (Ps. 111:6). So, should Gentile nations accuse Israel and say, 'You are robbers! You conquered and took a land which belonged to other people!' there is a good answer. The Jews can say, 'The whole earth is God's earth. He created it and He gives a country to whomsoever He wills. At first He gave the land to other nations;

and then in accordance with His will He took it away from them and gave it to us.'

For Rashi, and indeed in all classical rabbinic Judaism, the chief purpose of the Torah is to give Israel the Divine laws and teaching. In accordance with that view the commandments of the Torah are primary, and the historical narrative without the commandments is secondary. From that standpoint a good case can be made out for the Torah to have started with the very first commandment given to the whole of Israel, which was the commandment to observe the Passover in the month of Nisan.

The answer given here by Rashi is that at the very outset of the Bible the Torah wanted to establish Israel's right to the land of Canaan. The implication of the answer is that Israel's right to the land is basic and belongs to the entire concept of Israel as a separate people who became the recipients of all the commandments which were subsequently promulgated to them as the people of the Torah.

In essence, Rashi's comment is really *derush*, since one can argue that the account of God's creation calls for the belief that there is a God, and that He is the Creator. These are surely the first principles of religious faith, and it is therefore proper that the Bible should begin with the Creation story. In fact, Nahmanides (1194–1270) makes this point. Now Rashi must have been just as aware of that, and yet he introduces his *derush*. The likelihood is that Rashi's comment is a gentle polemic against the Christians. At the time of his writing the Christian holy places in Palestine were in the hands of the Muslims, and the Crusaders were planning to do battle with them to gain possession of the Holy Land. Rashi's comment is a reminder that the land belongs neither to the Muslims nor to the Christians. It was promised by God to Israel; and that promise will in time be fulfilled by the restoration of the land to Israel.

Rashi's *derush*, as usual, is not original. In fact he quotes here the saying of R. Isaac,[26] and the thrust of the *derush* is found in Midrash Bereshith Rabbah as well as in other midrashic collections. This, by the way, is a good illustration of how a student of Rashi, in the process of learning the commentary, will at the same time learn some Midrash.

In the beginning God created the heaven and the earth (ibid.).

> [RASHI] This verse simply calls out to be explained in accordance with the rabbinic exposition of the Midrash. There it is noted that the Torah is called *reshith*, 'the beginning', as in the verses, *The Lord made me [the Torah] as the beginning (reshith) of His way* (Prov. 8:22). Also, Israel is referred to as *reshith* as in the verse, *Israel is His first (reshith) fruits of the increase* (Jer. 2:3).
>
> However, if the *peshat* is preferred then understand the verse as follows: 'In the beginning of God's creating the heaven and the earth, the earth was unformed and void...' (*ibid.*, vv. 1–2).

Rashi starts off with an implied question. What is the meaning of the first Hebrew word of the Bible, *B'reshith*, usually translated 'In the beginning'? He gives us a *derush* and a *peshat*. This is frequently his method, except that here he submits the *derush* first. In making his point he offers the rabbinic homilies where *reshith*, 'the beginning', is the term for Torah (Bereshith Rabbah) and in another place (Leviticus Rabbah) it stands for Israel. This provides us with two interesting teachings. First, that God created the universe on the basis of the plan of Torah. Second, that He created it for the sake of Israel. In neither case does the *beth* prefix mean 'in': in the first homily it means 'with' and in the second it means 'for the sake of'. The significant ideas are clear. In the first it teaches that the whole of Creation depends on its being established on the teachings of Torah. Should that plan be upset then the world could not exist and all would be destroyed. The second homily can be connected with the idea of Israel's responsibility to redeem the world and all mankind by bringing it under the sovereignty of the only One God, Creator of all things.

In his *peshat* Rashi offers another translation of the first two verses. The fact is that, strictly speaking, the word *bereshith* does not mean 'In the beginning' because the Hebrew word means literally, 'In the beginning of...' But the accepted punctuation of the verse and the verse ending does not provide a noun which goes with the construct form *bereshith*. Therefore Rashi connects it with the second verse and translates, 'In the beginning of God's creation of the heaven and the earth, the earth was unformed and void...' This is a perfectly valid translation according to the *peshat* and is in fact followed by several modern translations of the Bible including the new translation of Torah by the Jewish Publication Society.

And on the seventh day God finished His work which He had made (Gen. 2:2).

> [RASHI] R. Simeon said: Ordinary mortals who cannot perceive the precise moment of correct time will often add from the end of one day to the beginning of the next, and to be absolutely certain that they do not desecrate the holy day they will have to add from the profane to the holy. Not so however with the Holy One blessed be He who knows the precise fraction of every moment. He allowed the work of Creation to continue till the exact second of the end of the sixth day although to the human eye it could appear that the work ceased after the seventh day had already started.
>
> Another explanation. After the Creation, all that was needed was rest. Thus the Sabbath day of rest came. Then it could be said that the work of Creation was truly completed on the seventh day when Sabbath came.

Again, Rashi replies to a question arising out of the text. The difficulty is obvious. Surely, God finished His work at the end of the sixth day and not on the seventh day as stated in the verse?

Rashi's reply follows the Midrash. His first explanation is an attempt at *peshat* which answers the question by suggesting that for God the work was really finished at the exact moment of the sixth day's end—something that the human eye could never perceive. His second answer is pure *derush* but here again it is absolutely in place. First of all it solves the problem of the text.

But it also gives us the beautiful lesson that the Sabbath rest was the final act of God's creation.

And God said unto Noah: 'The end of all flesh is come before Me: for the earth is filled with violence through them; and, behold, I will destroy them with the earth' (Gen. 6:13).

> [RASHI] *The end of all flesh.* Whenever society becomes degenerate through sexual immorality and idolatry it suffers destruction which kills the good as well as the wicked.
>
> *For the earth is filled with violence.* Their decree was not finally sealed until the evil of robbery became widespread.
>
> *With the earth.* The Hebrew particle *eth* here is the equivalent of 'trom'. We find examples of this usage as in the verse *As soon as I am gone out of* (Hebrew *eth*) *the city* (Ex. 9:29). Another explanation of the Hebrew *eth* is 'with' and here it literally means that man was destroyed *with* the earth which was ruined to a depth of three handbreadths below the surface of the ground.

Rashi notes that the doom is pronounced on *all* flesh, i.e. the innocent as well as the wicked. Noah and his family were to be the only exceptions. His comment suggests the inevitable fate of good citizens in a time of national pestilence when there is no escape even for the innocent.

In rabbinic teaching, the *corruption* (verse 12) of Noah's generation was in sexual immorality and idolatry. In the present verse the doom is pronounced on mankind because of their *violence* which is identified with robbery. In a sense this is even worse than the other two heinous offences described as *corruption*, because *violence* is a crime against one's fellow man. Therefore Rashi makes the telling point that in spite of *corruption*, i.e. sexual immorality and idolatry, mankind's destruction is not finally decreed until society is overtaken by *violence*, i.e. crimes of man against his fellow man.

Rashi's last comment on this verse deals with a simple point in Hebrew grammar. How do we translate the Hebrew particle *eth*? Mostly it simply precedes a noun in the accusative. But it can also mean 'from' or 'with'. Rashi gives examples of the first usage, and explains the validity of the second. His reference to the depth of three handbreadths takes note of the talmudic explanation that this is the extent of the maximum amount of earth that can be upturned by the strongest plough. Below that it is not *eretz*, earth.

And Noah went in, and his sons, and his wife, and his sons' wives with him, into the ark, because of the waters of the flood (Gen. 7:7).

> [RASHI] *Noah and his sons.* The men were separated from the women because they were not permitted marital relations while the whole world was in distress.
>
> *Because of the waters of the flood.* Even Noah was a man of insufficient faith. One day he believed that the flood would come and the next day he refused to believe it. As a matter of fact he did not enter the ark until he was forced to do so by the waters of the flood.

The text poses the question why the sexes are separated—Noah and his sons; his wife and his sons' wives. Rashi resolves the point by suggesting that marital relations between the sexes were prohibited during the flood. The source for this notion is found in Gen. 6:18 where the Divine command expressly states *And thou shalt come into the ark, thou and thy sons, and thy wife and thy sons' wives with thee.* The *peshat* is thus made clear—the sexes are separated and they entered the ark separately. But then Rashi adds the *derush* in supplying the reason—the whole world was in distress. Herein lies a beautiful teaching. When one's society is in trouble the individual cannot live a normal life as if nothing was happening outside. The good man is an involved man. At least he shares some of the pain and the deprivation of the society in which he lives.

Rashi offers a second comment on the verse in reply to the question why the text says that Noah entered the ark *because of the waters of the flood.* Surely they went in at God's command? But Rashi sees a deeper point in the phrase which connects Noah's entry into the ark with the onset of the flood. His comment also adds a descriptive touch to Noah's character.

And it came to pass after these things, that God did prove Abraham, and said to him: 'Abraham'; and he said: 'Here am I' (Gen. 22:1).

[RASHI] *After these things.* Some rabbis say that this took place after the words of Satan who criticized the patriarch before God and said, 'From all that big feast which Abraham made he did not sacrifice even a single bullock or ram to You.' God answered him, 'Abraham does everything for his son, and yet if I were to command him to offer up Isaac his son to Me, he would not refuse to do so.' Other rabbis say that the event took place after Ishmael's words when he boasted to Isaac that he (Ishmael) was circumcized when he was thirteen years old and he did not object to the pain. To this Isaac answered, 'You need not intimidate me. You were pained in only one limb. As far as I am concerned, if God were to order me to sacrifice my entire body and whole life to Him I would not protest against the command.'

Here am I. Such is the response of a pious man. It is an expression of humility and of readiness to do God's will.

A rabbinic exegesis maintains that the biblical phrase *And it came to pass after these things* introduces a new section which is connected with the previous chapter. Now the new section deals with the story of the binding of Isaac, and the connecting link with the previous chapter is to be found in the record of the banquet which Abraham made to celebrate the weaning of Isaac (Gen. 21:8).

Another point to be made is that the Hebrew word for 'things' is here *d'varim*, which can also mean 'words', i.e. 'speech'.

So the scene is set for Rashi's rabbinic folklore connecting God's command to Abraham with some prior words spoken after the feast which Abraham made to celebrate the growth of his precious son Isaac. This piece of folklore retells a fascinating rabbinic legend—the kind which the people loved. But of course it is pure *derush*. Nevertheless, and this is always important to remember, it is not *derush* introduced arbitrarily to tell a delightful story. It is submitted by Rashi because he needs it to explain the above two points, *After these things*, and 'things' meaning 'words'. The questions 'Which things?' 'What words?' are nicely answered by the rabbinic legends offered by Rashi, Satan's criticism and Ishmael's boast. The two legends possibly reflect the two opinions as to who is the central hero of the story, Abraham or Isaac. Interestingly, Rashi refrains from giving his own preference, and in the absence of his own opinion we might infer that he regards Abraham and Isaac as equally heroic and there is nothing to enable us to choose one before the other. This seems to be supported by his subsequent comments in verses 6 and 8.

And He said: 'Take now thy son, thine only son, whom thou lovest, even Isaac, and get thee up into the land of Moriah; and offer him there for a burnt offering upon one of the mountains which I will tell thee of' (Gen. 22:2).

> [RASHI] *Thy son.* Abraham said, 'But I have two sons.' So God said, *'Thine only son.'* To this Abraham parried, 'Each one is an only son: Ishmael to his mother Hagar, and Isaac to his mother Sarah.' God then added, *'Whom you love.'* But Abraham argued, 'I love them both.' So finally God explicitly said, *'Even Isaac.'*
>
> Now why did God give His command in such a long-drawn-out way? The answer is that God approached the matter gradually to avoid upsetting Abraham too suddenly. That would of course have happened had He abruptly ordered Abraham to sacrifice Isaac. Another reason was to give Abraham the opportunity to earn a spiritual reward for complying with each separate part of the Divine command.
>
> *The land of Moriah.* That is in Jerusalem. So we find in II Chr. 3:1, *The house of the Lord in Jerusalem in the mount of Moriah.* Our sages observed that the mount was so called because teaching (Hebrew, *horaah*) went out from there. The Onkelos Aramaic translation connects Moriah with myrrh (Hebrew *mor*), which was one of the spices used to make the incense burn during the ritual of the Temple service.

Rashi's commentary on this verse is another good example of *derush* which is introduced to answer a question in the text. The question is obvious. Why does God draw out His command in such a way? Could He not have ordered Abraham simply to offer up Isaac without prefacing the words, *thy son, thine only son, whom thou lovest*? The rabbinic legend of Abraham's conversation with God is a very touching story. But the details also fit in perfectly with the text.

Further, the lesson of the story is a good one, and Rashi probably had in mind the implied moral teaching that a man should avoid surprising his fellow with sudden unpleasant news. One should approach the subject gradually. It is a lesson on the value of tact and thoughtfulness.

The land of Moriah. The rabbinic identification of Moriah with the Temple mount is explained by Rashi in three succinct points. There is a verse in the Bible, the rabbis associate Moriah with *horaah* (teaching) and Onkelos connects it with *mor* (the spice myrrh). Thus in relatively few words the great commentator gathers together all the valid points which support the belief that the binding of Isaac took place on the site which was later to become the Temple mount.

Onkelos was a convert to Judaism who lived in the second century. Legend has it that he was a nephew of the Roman emperor. Onkelos's translation of the Bible into Aramaic was highly praised by the rabbis, and Rashi's frequent reliance on it is an illustration of the great esteem in which it was held as an accurate and faithful translation of the sacred text.

Now Moses was keeping the flock of Jethro his father-in-law, the priest of Midian, and he led the flock to the farthest end of the wilderness, and came to the mountain of God, unto Horeb (Ex. 3:1).

[RASHI] *The farthest end of the wilderness*. To avoid the possibility of theft, should the sheep stray to pasture in fields belonging to other people.

The mountain of God. So called with reference to its future.

This is a simple but clear example of Rashi's *peshat* which not only explains the meaning of a word or phrase but also gives its sense. Why did Moses have to go to the furthest part of the wilderness? Surely there were ample pasture areas in more accessible places! The answer which Rashi gives makes good sense and adds a description to the character portrayal of Moses as a man of strict justice.

The second point in Rashi's commentary on this verse faces the obvious question. Horeb was another name for Mount Sinai. But its description as *the mountain of God* is appropriate only after the great event of the Revelation of God on Sinai to declare the Ten Commandments (Ex. 19–20). How then could it be called *the mountain of God* at this early point in the story? Of course, the eleventh-century Rashi is unaware of anything like Bible criticism, but he sees the question and he comments briefly and simply that Moses wrote this later, giving Horeb the designation which it was subsequently to achieve.

Now these are the ordinances which thou shalt set before them (Ex. 21:1).

[RASHI] *Now these are the ordinances.* In every place where a scriptural passage begins with *these are* (i.e. without the conjunction *vav*) it indicates the start of a new section without any connection with the preceding passage. But where Scripture starts with *Now* ('and') *these are* (i.e. with the conjunctive *vav*) then it shows that it is the beginning of a new section which is connected with and adds something to the chapter that went before it. What is the connection here? Just as the previous section (the Ten Commandments) were proclaimed at Sinai, so too these laws were also given by God at Sinai.

Again, why is this section placed immediately after the laws dealing with the altar? (Ex. 20: 19–23) It is to teach that the house of the High Court shall be located in the Temple.

Which thou shalt set. God said to Moses: 'You should not think that all you will need to do is to teach the people a chapter or a law two or three times until they know it parrot fashion, without bothering to teach them to understand the reason and the meaning of the law.' Therefore Scripture underlines the phrase *which thou shalt set*, i.e. like a table which is set and all prepared for a meal.

Before them. And not before the courts of the heathen. And even if you know that in a certain case their law is like the Jewish law, nevertheless you should not submit the matter to their courts. For whoever brings the lawsuits of Israelites before their courts profanes God's name while honouring idol worshippers...

Rashi's first point deals with an important issue in Jewish thought. What is the source and authority for Jewish law? It would seem that even in early times the rabbis were aware that while the Jews recognized the Sinaitic and Divine authority of the Ten Commandments, there were some who were doubtful about the authority for the smaller laws and ordinances. Because of this, the rabbis put an end to the original practice of the daily reading of the Ten Commandments in the Temple, since they suspected that some people might get the impression that they were the only really important laws in Judaism since they were the only ones proclaimed by God on Sinai. In rabbinic Judaism every law in the Bible has its source in the Divine word, so it is not only the Ten Commandments which are authoritative: all the laws derive from God. In his first comment on our verse Rashi makes this teaching very clear. The chapter contains a miscellany of civil laws touching upon the treatment of slaves, damages to the person and to property—laws which are far removed from the fundamental and universal teaching of the Ten Commandments. Therefore, Rashi's comment, which connects the two kinds of law to the same Divine source, is of great theological importance. It is interesting that while Rashi quotes a Midrash (Ex. Rab. 30:1) his own comment is concise and much clearer than his midrashic source.

The few verses immediately before our present chapter deal with regulations for building an altar. Now in rabbinic exegesis there is a principle known as *semichuth* or juxtaposition: some rabbis argued that the fact that two subjects are recorded next to each other teaches something. What is the connection between the altar and the civil code of our chapter? Rashi notes that it means that the Sanhedrin was to be housed in the Temple precincts (some manuscripts read 'near to the altar'). Historically this is true: the Sanhedrin occupied a chamber in the Temple building known as *Lishkath Ha-gazith*—the Chamber of Hewn Stones. Rashi may have found significance in this since it would be a constant reminder to the judges that the pursuit of justice and its dispensation is a form of Divine worship.

Rashi's comments on the phrase *which thou shalt set before them* are interesting. The phrase 'to set' the law before the people is unusual in itself since in most other places we read about God instructing Moses to 'speak' to the people telling them the laws. 'Setting' the laws thus calls for a special note, and here Rashi explains the phrase as only one like him could explain it, that is, from his own experience as a good teacher.[27]

His final reference to the place of the Jewish court calls for a few brief observations. Rashi lived in a Christian community. Like other great Jewish teachers he does not regard Christians as heathens or idol worshippers. Moreover, in his day Jewish courts had autonomy and authority, frequently officially granted to them by the civil powers. It is more than likely then that, generally speaking, Jews took their legal disputes to their own rabbinic courts for settlement, either for religious reasons or for purely economic considerations, being reluctant to divulge their assets to the civic authorities. Nevertheless, one cannot avoid the suspicion that Rashi's comment under this heading suggests that occasionally Jews might have resorted to the Gentile courts instead of putting their case before their rabbis for a decision.

Rashi's commentary on this verse is characteristic of his work on the legal sections of the Bible. In these chapters there is no *derush*, or very little of it, and his writing has the single aim of explaining the *peshat* of the text and the meaning of the law.

If thou buy a Hebrew servant, six years he shall serve; and in the seventh he shall go out free for nothing (Ex. 21:2).

[RASHI] *If thou buy a Hebrew servant.* This law relates to a servant who is himself a Hebrew. Do not think that the law applies to a Canaanite servant whom you bought from a Hebrew master, and that such a servant works for six years only, while one bought from a Canaanite master may be in permanent service in accordance with the verse, *And ye may make them an inheritance for your children after you, to hold for a possession* (Lev. 25:46). Such an inference is incorrect since we have the verse, *If thy brother, a Hebrew man, or a Hebrew woman, be sold unto thee, he shall serve thee six years* (Deut. 15:12). So we can apply the exegetical rule which allows us to learn from the similarity of words ('Hebrew') that just as in Deuteronomy the verse describes the servant as *thy brother*, i.e. himself a Hebrew, so too in our verse here the law relates also to the *Hebrew servant* who is also *thy brother*, i.e. is himself a Hebrew.

The Hebrew phrase *eved ivri*, 'a Hebrew servant', can also mean a servant of a Hebrew; i.e. a non-Hebrew who belonged to a Hebrew master. With such a reading the Bible would here be stating that the six-year law applies to such a servant. Hence Rashi's need to clarify that it applies only to one who is himself a Hebrew.

The exegetical principle which Rashi invokes is called *gezerah shavah* and is the second of Rabbi Ishmael's famous thirteen principles according to which the rabbis expound and extend the many meanings and inferences in the Bible text. The *gezerah shavah* is based on the principle of similarity of language in two verses. Thus, consider two cases, A and B, which deal with similar situations and which employ, at least in part, the same terminology or word. If the description in A is defective while in case B it is full and explicit, then all doubts about case A are resolved by applying to it all the details of case B. So in our present verse we read the law of the six years for a 'Hebrew servant', but we are not sure whether the servant is himelf a Hebrew or simply one acquired from a Hebrew master. Then in Deuteronomy we again read of the six-year rule; but this time it applies to *thy brother a Hebrew*. There it is explicit and very clear; the Hebrew we are talking about is *thy brother*; i.e. he is himself a

Hebrew. Then with the help of the *gezerah shavah* principle we are able to say that, just as in Deuteronomy the term 'Hebrew' relates to the servant himself, in our present verse in Exodus the term 'Hebrew' also relates to the servant himself.

But if the servant shall say... I will not go out free; then his master shall bring him unto God (the judges), and shall bring him to the door, or unto the door-post; and his master shall bore his ear through with an awl; and he shall serve him forever (Ex. 21:5–6).

[RASHI] *Unto God.* To the Court. Since it is only right that he consult those who sold him.

To the door, or unto the door-post. The two-fold phrase of 'door' and 'door-post' is explained as follows: You might think that the door-post is the proper place for piercing the ear; hence Scripture indicates elsewhere (Deut. 15:17) *into the door,* i.e. the door and not the door-post. In that case why include door-post in our present verse at all? It is in order to compare the door to it in this important respect. Just as the door-post is upright so the door must also be upright at the time of the piercing... Now why is the ear a more appropriate place to be pierced than any other limb of the servant's body? Rabbi Johanan ben Zakkai taught: The ear heard from Sinai *Thou shalt not steal* (Ex. 20:15) and this man went and stole—then let his ear be pierced. In the case of a man who sold himself into servitude, again we can say, it was the ear which heard from Sinai, *For unto Me the children of Israel are servants* (Lev. 15:55) and this man went and acquired another master for himself, let his ear be pierced. Rabbi Simeon expounded the verse in a delightful way. He said: How is the door or door-post different from all other items in the house? God said: 'The door and the door-post were witnesses in Egypt when I passed over the lintel and the door-posts and proclaimed, *For unto Me the children of Israel are servants* (ibid.), i.e. *My* servants and not the servants of servants. Then this man went and acquired another master for himself! Let his ear be pierced in their presence.'

And he shall serve him forever. This means till the Jubilee year. Should you think that this could mean that 'forever' is to be taken literally, then we are put right by another verse (Lev. 25:10) which states, *And ye shall return every man to his family* at the Jubilee year and from which we can learn that the Hebrew term *l'olam* 'forever' in our verse can only mean until the year of the Jubilee. Nor should we think that the law means that the servant shall serve fifty years, until he completes his own Jubilee. Not at all: it means that he remains in servitude only until the national Jubilee, whether it is close or far off.

The servant who refuses to go free at the end of his six years of service is given a mark of shame because of his rejection of the value of freedom. But first of all he is brought before the court for consultation. The Hebrew word *elohim* is given the translation in the J.P.S. Bible of 'God', with a note that it means 'judges' (see also Ex. 22:8). Rashi here straightaway gives the obvious *peshat*, which is 'judges', but in addition he tells us why the judges are brought into the picture. It is because this man was sold by the court to pay off his theft and his fine. This is one reason for a Hebrew to be found in servitude. The other way in which a man can be a servant is if he sells himself on account of his extreme poverty. Now the Bible deals with such a case in a separate passage (Lev. 25:39–42), so this verse deals with the man who stole and was sold by the court. In such a case it is reasonable that the judges be consulted first if the man refuses to go into freedom when his opportunity to do so arises. Rashi thus gives us the *peshat* and then adds a reason for the law.

To the door, or unto the door-post. Rashi here gives a typical talmudic argument from which we learn that the door-post is excluded from being a place where the ear is pierced. It is only included in our verse in order to compare it to the door which, like the door-post, has to be in an upright position.

Rashi's next comment sounds like good rabbinic *derush*, but on closer examination one can see that it is introduced here because through it we get a deeper understanding of the biblical law in answer to the questions, 'Why is it to be the ear which is pierced?' and 'Why is it done against the door?'

And he shall serve him forever. Rashi makes two points here, in both cases with the Talmud as his source. First, that the term 'forever' means until the Jubilee year. It is perhaps arguable that Rashi could have found a more explicit biblical reference, not in Leviticus 25:10 but in the same chapter, verses 39–41, where it clearly states that the servant shall serve only until the Jubilee year and then he goes out with his family into freedom. Perhaps the answer is that the latter section deals with one who has sold himself on account of his poverty while our present verse deals, as we have seen, with one who was sold by the court. In any case the law of the termination of servitude in the Jubilee year is the same for both classes of servants. The second point made here by Rashi is that the servant does not serve until he has completed his own term of fifty years or his own personal 'jubilee' but until the national Jubilee year when every one in ancient Hebrew society had a new economic start in life.

4

THE TALMUD COMMENTARY

I

The Bible, or the Written Law, was always the primary source of Judaism. But Judaism does not rest on the Bible alone, rather on the Bible as it has been interpreted throughout history. Every student of Judaism knows this. The following necessarily simplified summary will help to make the matter clear to other readers.

First of all, there are laws and teachings in the Bible which in the course of history were declared by the leading and authoritative rabbis to be no longer relevant and therefore, for all practical purposes, were taken out of normative Judaism. Secondly, there are many current Jewish religious laws and customs which are not mentioned in the Bible at all. It is as if, from the point of view of the Scriptures, those newer laws were not part of biblical Judaism. Thirdly, there are countless teachings in the Bible which cannot be understood, and never were understood, in accordance with their simple literal meaning. That is to say that, on their own, those biblical laws were not incorporated into practical Judaism without a traditional explanation which went hand in hand with the written text of the Bible. Let us briefly take a few examples under each of the three categories to illustrate these basic facts about the sources of Judaism.

Our first point can be illustrated by reference to the laws of the Sabbatical Year (Deut. 15:1–2). According to the biblical regulations, in every seventh year all debts were to be annulled and the debtor released from his obligation to the creditor. Undoubtedly, there was a very ethical concept in the promulgation of such a law. Among other things, it gave the poor man a new chance to rebuild his life and to lift himself up from a situation of dire poverty. In an early pastoral economy, the law of release in the Sabbatical Year was of great benefit to the underprivileged class while encouraging the virtue of charity in those more fortunate. However, in the course of time and with the change from a pastoral to a commercial economy, such a law became impractical. The rich stopped lending as they saw the Sabbatical Year approaching, so that the man in real need could not obtain the help which he desperately required. Seeing how the entire economy of the community was badly affected, the first-century sage Hillel, the master-builder of rabbinic Judaism, overcame the problem by giving the biblical law a new interpretation which allowed the courts to collect the debt on behalf of the creditor—even in the Sabbatical Year. Another example in the same class of rabbinic expositions which virtually annulled a clear biblical law is found in connection with the law of the trial with the waters of bitterness ordained for the woman suspected of adultery (Num. 5:11–31). In the same century as Hillel there lived another outstanding sage and leader, Rabbi Johanan ben Zakkai. He proclaimed that the entire regulation dealing with the trial by the ordeal of the bitter waters was no longer applicable. He gave a number of valid reasons and arrived at his decision through a process of reinterpreting the biblical ordinance. It is clear that the new economic conditions at the time of Hillel and the new ethical and social sensitivities which were prevalent in the time of Johanan ben Zakkai motivated those teachers; but whatever the reasons, and whatever the principles of new interpretation which those rabbis adopted, the simple fact remains that a number of explicit laws of the Written Law were changed by the Oral Law.

Next, we saw that there are many laws and customs which are rooted in Jewish law and practice but which have no mention at all in the Bible itself. Lighting the Sabbath and Festival candles on the eve of the holy days is a universal Jewish practice, and the festival of Hanukkah is one of the most popular festivals in the Jewish Calendar. Yet neither the Sabbath candles nor the Hanukkah Festival is mentioned in the Bible. It is interesting that when the candles are lit, on both occasions, the

Jew thanks and praises God with the words, 'Who commanded us to kindle the lights of Sabbath (or Hanukkah).' Where did God so command? The answer of course is that it all derives from rabbinic interpretation of the Bible.

Finally, there are countless laws in the Bible which cannot be understood as written, and in fact were never accepted in their literal meaning. Almost every law in the Bible contains at least some evidence of this. Thus, the Bible forbids work on the Sabbath. Question: What constitutes work? It is not such a simple matter. What one man may think of as work, say, whitewashing his garden wall, another man may think of as great fun. Is it work to write a love letter? Is it work to plant a rose? Or what about turning on the radio to listen to one's favourite symphony? The Bible says absolutely nothing about such things, and we have to rely on rabbinic interpretation. Only there can we find a definition of 'work'. Let us take another example in this group. On the Festival of Tabernacles the Jew rejoices with palm branch and the fruit of the 'goodly tree' (Lev. 33:40). Now what on earth is this so-called fruit of the 'goodly tree'? Is it an apple? A fig? A cluster of grapes? Anyone is free to make his guess. But if he chooses any one of those fruits he would be in error. For the rabbis decided that the Bible intends the *etrog*, or citrus fruit. One could fill a thick book with such instances.

As we have indicated, we call the Bible the Written Law and the vast corpus of interpretation and tradition is known as the Oral Law. In rabbinic theology, the Oral Law is authoritative and even partakes of the Divine in its initial source. We can think of the Oral Law as the extended arm of the Written Law and it cannot be separated from it since they are ultimately parts of the same body of Divine teaching.

For a long time, as the name in fact implies, the Oral Law remained an unwritten code. It is likely that the rabbis insisted that it remain unwritten because, as new circumstances required, there would be a better chance that the Oral Law would remain fluid enough to absorb all nuances, changes and shifts of emphasis. The interpretation would therefore always be dynamic, even as life itself is dynamic.

However, after the destruction of the Second Temple in the year 70 CE, and the world-wide dispersion of the Jewish people, conditions of life for the Jews entered a new and dangerous period. Their very survival as a nation was in question. They were now without a country, without a Temple, without a king and without a High Priest. There was no longer a geographical point or figure of authority to hold them together as a separate or distinctive people. At this critical point in Jewish life rabbinic leaders recognized that the scattered Jewish communities could still be held together in a meaningful unity by loyalty to the faith of Judaism and disciplined observance of its laws. These would not only sanctify the life of the Jews but would also serve as a unifying culture which would bind Jews together into a single people wherever they lived. Without a land there would still be a loyalty to a centralizing value; without kings there would still be a sense of dignity and high prestige in their lives; without a Temple there would still be sanctity in the life of every Jew; and without a High Priest every Jew would function as a priest in his own home which would become like a miniature temple. But this new policy and programme necessitated that the people be given clear and detailed directions. This in turn meant that the Oral Law, which until then had remained in its unwritten and uncodified form, had to be gathered together and arranged into a systematic code. This massive work was finally accomplished by Rabbi Judah the Prince in the year 200 CE, and it was the most important step in putting into order the vast treasury of the oral teachings and traditions of Judaism. This work of Judah is called the Mishnah and it is divided into six encyclopaedic volumes which together cover all aspects of Jewish religious life up to the time of its redaction.

But the Mishnah, while it is the most important part of the Oral Law, now in its written form, is only one part of it. Judah's Mishnah at once became the subject of intensive, critical and detailed examination, in the Palestinian and Babylonian academies. These extensive discussions were also written down and are called the Gemara. The Mishnah and the Gemara together comprise the Talmud. Since there were rabbinic academies in Palestine and in Babylon, and since the rabbinic discussions went on—almost independently of each other—in both countries, there are naturally two Gemaras to Judah's Mishnah. Hence we talk about two Talmuds, the Jerusalem Talmud and the Babylonian Talmud. Because of the impoverished and persecuted condition of Palestinian Jewry, by the beginning of the fourth century the academies were closing down and more and more of the Palestinian scholars emigrated. The Jerusalem Talmud remained unfinished and nothing further was added to it after about 325 CE. The Babylonian academies flourished for much longer and the Babylonian Talmud was finished in the year 500 with the decision of the rabbis not to add any more to the talmudic text.

Next to the Bible, the Babylonian Talmud then became the authoritative source for Jewish law and life. It embodies the entire spectrum of classical Jewish beliefs, concepts, value systems and the detailed description of Jewish law under every heading of human experience. To navigate this ocean of rabbinic literature requires the skill and the acumen of experience and scholarship. In our own time the task is made much easier with the numerous studies on the Talmud which have brought light and interpretation to almost every page of the difficult text. There are also translations into every popular language so that the student who is unfamiliar with the difficult Aramaic language of the Gemara can usually find his way through the text. In Rashi's time, the situation was entirely different. There were no translations into Hebrew or into any other language. Further, not only is the text of the Talmud itself very difficult, but, in addition, the transmission of the Talmud text had always been problematic; the student was frequently faced with the question whether the text in front of him was authentic or defective. But the first and constant problem for the student was in fact to decipher the actual meaning of the difficult text. It is here that Rashi showed his genius. He provided his students with the most comprehensive and clearest explanation of the Talmud. Without his commentary it is not unlikely that the Talmud would have remained a neglected book. We must now examine this extraordinary work a little more closely in order to understand the unique and massive contribution of Rashi to Jewish learning.

II

When we compare the Rashi commentaries on the Bible and the Talmud we immediately see the clear difference in style and approach. The Bible commentary can be said to have been written for the masses. While it aims to give the meaning of the text, it is liberally interspersed with legend and homily. The Bible commentary appealed to the heart, and the Bible—particularly the Pentateuch—with Rashi's commentary was a popular work for the people: it was part of the regular school curriculum and became the staple reading text in every pious Jewish home.

Not so the Talmud commentary. Here we are dealing with a basic rabbinic text which is riddled with problems that have to be solved in order to arrive at its true meaning. Rashi's commentary on the Talmud necessarily appeals therefore to the intellect. It is a work for the serious student who struggles to unravel the talmudic complexities in his search for the meaning of the text. Other works had preceded Rashi's, at least in partial commentaries, but none had really succeeded. Some of them were too profuse; others too concise. Most of them failed to solve the riddle of the enigmatic text. Rashi's commentary is acknowledged as the first to provide a key to the mysteries of the vast storehouse of the talmudic writings.

The difficulties of understanding the Talmud derive from several factors. First of all there is the question of language. While the Mishnah is in Hebrew, the Gemara is written in Aramaic, the language spoken by Jews both in Palestine and in Babylon during the centuries which spanned the composition of the Talmud. For the Jews in France and Germany, Aramaic was virtually a foreign language. It says a great deal for the intellectual standards of the Jewry of those countries that their leaders, rather than withdrawing into scholarly isolation, insisted on making the difficult text of the Talmud a central subject of study in their communities.

Secondly, there is no punctuation, so a non-expert cannot easily tell where one sentence ends and another begins; what is a question and what is a simple statement. Further, the discussion is extremely fluid and a subject is frequently broken off while the Talmud proceeds for several pages with the exposition of an entirely different subject which may have no relevance, or very little relevance, to the subject of the first discussion. In addition to all this, students of the Talmud in Rashi's day would have had a serious problem in deciding on the accurate text of the Talmud. Unlike the Bible, there was no masoretic tradition to give its seal of authenticity to the Talmud text. The problem was aggravated by the careless errors of copyists; worse still, not a few copyists sought to 'improve' the text with their own emendations. As we have already noted, Rabbenu Gershom of Mainz saw this as a major problem in Talmud studies and he therefore laboured hard to produce what he regarded as the final, corrected, complete and authentic text of the Talmud. Rashi himself had access to this and he relied heavily on Gershom's text.[1] Nevertheless, he frequently suggests alternative readings—'We should read thus,' he says, in places where it seems to him that a slight emendation would give the text its proper meaning—but those observations are in his commentary itself. Rashi never alters the text of the Talmud, although in many cases subsequent copyists incorporated his emendations into the Talmud text and in time the Rashi text of the Talmud became the official, or at least the generally acknowledged, text.

Accepting all the difficulties of the Talmud's language and the rabbinic discussion, Rashi dedicates himself to the single task of making its meaning clear. He injects himself into the text, identifying question and statement, explaining words and phrases, making sense of an argument or a point in the discussion. In his pursuit of *peshat* he has no time for the hair-splitting arguments and the minor subtleties which were the stock-in-trade of other commentators. In fact, he is often very critical of them and maintains that they only bring confusion to an already difficult subject.[2]

There are many parallel passages in the Talmud, but in his commentaries Rashi rarely repeats the same explanation: when his explanations of two parallel passages amount to the same thing, they are worded differently. He never says the same thing twice in the same language. There is usually a divergence of style, in the arrangements of his comments or in the length of his explanations. This might have been deliberate, an affectation of style. On the other hand, it might be due to the fact that in large part his Talmud commentary was based on his oral teaching, so there is a certain fluidity of style and approach. Occasionally there is a difference in the explanations of parallel passages and this is undoubtedly due to Rashi's revision of his work in which he deliberately introduced changes or shifted his emphasis. We know that he revised his commentaries several times and that he constantly strove for ever greater accuracy and lucidity.

Rashi's Talmud commentary covers most of the treatises. But there are several treatises where there is no Gemara following the Mishnah. These volumes have no Rashi commentary.[3] We have already noted that from Baba Batra page 29a to the end is not commented upon by Rashi. The commentary is that of his grandson Rashbam, possibly with the addition of the comments of other scholars. We have also noted that he died before completing his commentary on treatise Makkoth; the commentary in that volume, from 19b, was written by Judah ben Nathan. In addition, there are a number of other treatises about which there is some doubt whether the commentaries are the work of Rashi or of later scholars.[4]

Evaluations of Rashi's commentary always consist of barely qualified praise. The few points of criticism are usually associated with Rashi's ignorance of subjects such as history or geography, where his commentaries usually show that his knowledge of these subjects was even less than elementary.[5] But in this respect Rashi was merely a child of his age, when scientific knowledge was quite outside the purview of most scholars. Again, a modern scholar may find it strange that Rashi seems to confuse legend with history and accepts the record of rabbinic folklore as a description of factual events. Here, too, we would do well to remember that Rashi is a typical pious Jew of the eleventh century, for whom the legends and folklore of the Talmud were read as history. This was the unquestioned belief of Rashi's generation and it would be wrong to criticize him for not being another Maimonides. The great Spanish philosopher lived a century after

Rashi and he worked in an entirely different milieu. We can judge Rashi's work only against the background of his age and the terms of reference which he set for himself. This was essentially to give the *peshat* and explain the meaning of the Talmud text. Against that declared aim Rashi's commentary on the Talmud is incomparable. For generations before him most students of the Talmud found the work incomprehensible: Rashi was the one who broke the code of the rabbinic text. Rashi's brilliant grandson, Jacob ben Meir, known as Rabbenu Tam, is on record as having said that, while he might have been able to write a Bible commentary like his grandfather, he could never have produced anything like his grandfather's extraordinary work on the Talmud. That was unique.[6]

The uniqueness of the Talmud commentary also lies in the fact that, unlike his Bible commentary, it is for the mature scholar as well as for the layman. Even experienced and highly capable talmudic students still have need of Rashi's commentary. A commentary on a classic is needed to clarify the work for a generation of readers far removed from the original, but the commentary itself will become outdated in the course of time. It is acceptable, then, that there was a real need for successive commentaries on the Bible. But even modern readers need Rashi's commentary on the Talmud. No modern student of the Talmud will say, 'Let me see what the eleventh-century scholar from Troyes has to say!'—he will go to Rashi's commentary as if it were, with obvious exceptions, written as a timeless guide. In this respect it is different from all other medieval commentaries and even from his Bible commentary.

Rashi's work as Talmud commentator was continued by a group of scholars known as tosaphists (literally 'supplementers') founded by Rashi's disciples, who included his own grandchildren. For about two hundred years following Rashi they and their successors continued to add commentaries to the Talmud text, frequently taking up a point of explanation given by Rashi. In all standard editions of the Talmud the comments of the tosaphists appear in the outside column of each page, with Rashi's commentary printed in the inside column. It is noteworthy that Rashi's commentary is frequently referred to by the tosaphists as the *Kuntrus*, that is, 'the commentary'—as if there were really only one.

The most outstanding tosaphists were Samuel ben Meir (Rashbam); Jacob ben Meir (Rabbenu Tam), the most famous of Rashi's grandsons; Rabbenu Yitchak, a great-grandson; Yitchak ben Asher; Rabbenu Chaim; Rabbenu Peretz; and Meir of Rothenberg (1215–93), the acknowledged rabbinic scholar and community leader.

III

In this section we will give a few examples of Rashi's commentary on the Talmud. The first thing to note is the absence of *derush*: with the Talmud, Rashi's sole aim is to make the text intelligible. As we have tried to explain, Rashi takes the words and the phrases whose meanings are difficult and opens up the *peshat* for the student. His commentary is thus the key to the understanding of the text. In our examples the Mishnah and the Gemara are reproduced in a simple translation, with Rashi's comments in italic type within parentheses and following the word or phrase which he chooses to explain.

Our first example is the opening Mishnah and its Gemara in the first tractate of the Talmud, Berachoth. The subject deals with the time for reading the evening Shema. What is the first moment when it can be read and what is the *terminus ad quem*? The biblical rule that the Shema (Deut. 6:4–9, 11:13–21 and Num. 15:37–41) has to be read morning and evening is inferred from the Bible itself (*when thou liest down and when thou risest up*[7]) and the Talmud is here concerned with the time limits implied in the phrase *when thou liest down*, in other words, what is the proper time for reading the night-time Shema?

> [MISHNAH, Berachoth, 2a]   From what time may one read the evening Shema? From the time when the priests go home to eat their terumah[8] food [*priests who were ritually unclean and have immersed themselves are then permitted to eat the terumah food as soon as that day is over*]

until the end of the first watch [*which is one third of the night, as will be later explained in the Gemara. After that it is too late since it is no longer the time of 'lying down'. Similarly, one who reads the Shema before that time has not yet fulfilled his religious obligation. In that case, why do we read it early in the Synagogue?*[9] *Presumably, as we learn from a baraita*[10] *in the Jerusalem Talmud, it is in order to be able to read the Amidah prayer immediately after reading from the Scriptures. Hence it is proper to read the Shema again after dark. However, a man fulfils his religious obligation by reading the Shema, as is customary, on going to bed at night, even though he reads only the first paragraph*]. This is the view of R. Eliezer. The sages say that it may be read until midnight. Rabban Gamaliel rules that it may be read even until dawn [*since he believes that the entire night is 'lying down time'*].

It once happened that Rabban Gamaliel's sons came home late from a wedding feast and they told their father, 'We have not yet read the evening Shema.' The rabbi said to them, 'If dawn has not yet risen it is your duty to read it. Moreover in this as well as in all other cases where the sages teach that a ritual may be performed only until midnight, the law really permits it to be performed right until the dawn.' Thus the burning of the surplus fats and those parts cut away from the sacrifices [*whose blood was sprinkled as a sacrifice on that day*] can be carried out throughout the entire night. [*They can be burned on the altar all through the night and nothing is disqualified until it is dawn and has not been put on the altar fire: in accordance with the law, he shall not leave any of it until the morning.*[11] *And all this is learned from the laws of the thanksgiving offering.*] So too the meat of all sacrifices which has to be eaten during the day of the sacrifice may be eaten right up till the dawn on the following day. In that case why do the sages rule that the commandment has to be carried out by midnight [*e.g., the reading of the night-time Shema and the eating of the sacrificial meat*]? It is merely to provide a hedge and keep the man away from over-stepping the permitted time and so committing a transgression. [*The rabbis wanted to prevent*

*the eating of the sacrificial meat before it was really prohibited in
law, in order to make it even less likely that he would eat it after
dawn and so incur the penalty of Divine punishment. Similarly
in the case of the night-time reading of the Shema, the rabbis
want to hurry a man to the timely performance of his religious
duty. He should not say 'I have plenty of time,' and the dawn
come making it too late for him to read the Shema.*]

[GEMARA, Berachoth, 2a]   Why does the tanna[12] start
with the question 'From when?' when we don't yet know
that there is a rule to read the Shema? [*What is the basis for
the tanna's primary teaching that there is a law to read the
Shema, since in our Mishnah the tanna assumes this, so that he
can pose the question about the time for its reading.*] Another
question. Where is the logic in discussing the night-time
reading before he teaches about the morning Shema? The
answer is that the tanna bases himself on the biblical verse
[*from which he is able to derive the principle law that the Shema
shall be read*]... *when thou liest down and when thou risest
up*[13] and he expounds as follows: This reading of the
Shema at the 'lying down' time, when is it? And he
answers that the time is indicated by the practice of the
priests who, at the beginning of the night, go home to eat
their terumah. If you wish you can have another answer
[*why the tanna begins with a rule about the evening Shema*]. It
is because the tanna finds support from the story of the
Creation where the Bible records, *And there was evening
and there was morning, one day.*[14] An objection is now
raised. Why then does the tanna subsequently go on to
give the ruling that before the morning Shema two
blessings are read and one blessing after it; while in the case
of the evening Shema there are two blessings before and
two blessings after. The tanna should be consistent and give
us the rule about the evening Shema first. The answer is that
first [*in our Mishnah*] the tanna teaches about the evening
Shema: then in the next Mishnah he proceeds to give the
rule about the morning Shema [*i.e., From what time may one
read the morning Shema?*]. Then within the context of his

discussion of the morning Shema he goes on to tell about the blessings which precede and follow the morning Shema.

The subject of lost and found property has its source in the Bible and is represented in detailed legislation in tractate Baba Mezia. The following excerpts are from the opening section of that tractate. Rashi's comments on this passage provide a good example of his concern to make clear both the text and the argument.

[MISHNAH, Baba Mezia, 2a]   Two men appear before the court holding a garment. [*The law applies only if they are both physically holding the object, so that no one has more title to it than the other. However, if only one of them holds it, then the other is in the status of one who seeks to take possession of something which is already in the possession of another. In such a case he has to bring witnesses to support his claim, and his oath alone is not good enough.*] This one says, 'I found it,' and the other one says, 'I found it.' This one says, 'It is all mine,' and the other one says, 'It is all mine.' [*the Gemara will explain why the Mishnah formulates the separate parts of the claims in this way.*] The law is that each one of them shall swear [*the Gemara will explain the need for an oath in this case*] that his share in the found article is no less than half [*The Gemara will explain the apparently odd style of the oath*][15] and they then divide the value of the article beween them.

If one of them claims 'It is all mine' while the other one says 'Half belongs to me' [*the second man admits that half the article belongs to the first man so that the dispute is really only about the ownership of the second half. Hence the contested half is treated like the disputed whole in the first case and therefore each one will swear that his share in the contested part is no less than half of it*] the law is that the one who claims the entire object shall then swear that he is entitled to no less than three-quarters of it, while the second man will swear that his share in it is no less than a quarter: and they divide it up in that proportion.

If two men were riding [*this example comes to teach that the rider and the one who holds the reins have the same title to acquire the ownerless animal*] on an animal; or one was riding and the other was leading it. This one says, 'It is all mine,' and the other says, 'It is all mine.' Then each of them shall swear that he has no less than half ownership of the animal and then they shall divide its value.

In the case of admission [*later on the Gemara explains that this includes the situation of the finder who takes hold of an ownerless object to acquire it for someone else*] or if there is evidence of witnesses, then the division or disposition of the found article is made without imposing an oath.

[GEMARA, Baba Mezia, 2a]   What need is there for the Mishnah to record, This one says 'I found it' and the other one says 'I found it.' This one says 'It is all mine' and the other one says 'It is all mine'? Let each of them make one plea. In fact there is only one plea and we should read as follows: This one says, 'I found it and it is all mine' and the other one says, 'I found it and it is all mine.' But why doesn't the Mishnah simply state that the plea of each one is simply 'I found it' and we would understand from that claim that it also includes the claim 'It is all mine'? The answer is that had the Mishnah stated only 'I found it' I might have inferred that it means 'I saw it' [*before you picked it up*] and that an item may thus be acquired merely by seeing it [*since the ruling is that they share it*] even though the person does not actually take hold of it. Therefore the additional claim 'It is all mine' [*through actually holding it. 'I picked it up first and then you pulled it away from me after I had already taken possession of it'*] is necessary to make it clear that seeing alone does not constitute a claim.

Now can one really say that the claim 'I found it' can mean, as you seem to suggest, 'I saw it'? Did not Rabnai say [*in the tenth chapter of Baba Kama, 113b*] that the text *And thou has found it*[16] means that thou hast taken hold of it? [*If he had not taken hold of it he is not obligated to return it. But once he has taken hold of it he is duty bound to return it because he is prohibited from keeping lost property.*] True. The biblical expression *And thou has found* does mean to take hold. But the tanna is here using popular language [*had the Mishnah not included the additional claim 'It is all mine', I could have assumed that the phrase 'I found it' is used in the popular sense and not according to the precise meaning of the Bible. In the popular meaning people think that seeing alone is finding*] where a man only has to see an ownerless object and will claim 'I found it.' In such a situation although he did not take hold of it he might still think that he has acquired a right to it through merely seeing it. Hence the Mishnah adds the additional claim 'It is all mine' to indicate that seeing alone does not give a man right of possession...

Shall we assume that our Mishnah does not follow the view of ben Nanas who argued that we cannot impose an oath in a case where there is going to be a false oath. [*In tractate Shavuoth 45a where the law is that both sides to a claim swear before the judges even though we know that one is going to swear falsely. The case dealt with is that of a man who says to a storekeeper, 'Sell a dinar's worth of wheat to my son, and I will pay.' Or he says, 'Give my workman goods to the value of a sela which I owe in wages, and I will pay you.' The storekeeper then says, 'I gave them the goods,' but the others say, 'I got nothing.' The law is that the storekeeper and workman have to swear that they are entitled to the money, and the first man pays both. Ben Nanas argued against such a ruling because it involves one of them swearing falsely. So he rules that they both get their money without having to swear.*] Not at all. Our Mishnah can in fact be reconciled to the view of ben Nanas. For in the above case there is the certainty that one of the claimants is lying and we therefore know that his oath will be a false oath. Therefore in such a situation we do not impose an oath. But in our Mishnah there is no certainty that there will be a false oath if we assume that each claimant picked up the object. [*i.e., the found article. Each one believes that he took hold of it first, and therefore it is all*

his. *In such a case when each one swears that he has title to no
less than half, he swears truthfully . . .*]

Shall we say that our Mishnah does not follow the view
of Symmachus who holds that property whose ownership
is in doubt should be divided between the claimants
without an oath? [*This view is found in Baba Kama 46a in the
case of an ox which gores a cow and a dead newly born calf was
found beside the cow.*] So what would you say, that our
Mishnah follows the view of the sages? But they hold that
the burden of evidence falls on the one who is attempting
to extract something from another. [*In which case the
claimant has to produce witnesses in order to get anything; while
our Mishnah rules that both men share the article after taking an
oath.* (Rashi here then gives what he believes is the correct
text of the Gemara, which was incorporated by the copyist
into the regular text).] What sort of argument is this? You
can still say that our Mishnah follows the sages but that the
two cases are entirely different. Their view that the burden
of evidence falls on the one who is trying to get something
from another, applies only when neither of them is
holding on to the disputed object. But the case in our
Mishnah speaks of both holding on to the found object [*so
this is not a situation of one trying to take something from
another*] therefore they divide it up on oath. [*Since there is
no other way in which one can lawfully collect what the other
claimant holds while each one holds on to the entire article and
there are no witnesses. Therefore the sages impose an oath.*] But
you cannot say that the Mishnah is in accord with
Symmachus because if he holds that the disputed property
is divided without an oath in a situation where neither side
has hold on it, how much more emphatically would he
have the same opinion in a situation like the one in our
Mishnah where both claimants have hold on the article.
Nevertheless one can still reconcile the Mishnah to
Symmachus, for when does he rule that the claimants
divide the property without oath—only when neither can
be certain that he is the sole owner of the property. [*For
example, in the case cited above. A dead calf is lying beside the*

mother cow who has been gored by an ox. We do not know if the mother cow was gored before the calf was born (in which case the owner of the ox would have to pay also for the dead calf), *or if the calf was born before its mother was gored and the calf died from natural causes. Since each claim is one of doubt it is pointless to impose an oath.*] But in a case where each one claims with a certainty that he is the sole owner then Symmachus would agree that there shall be an oath.

Then what answer can be found for Rabbah bar R. Hanna who says [*Baba Mezia, 100a*] that Symmachus holds the same opinion, viz., that property is divided without oath even if both contending parties claim ownership with certainty? One can still relate our Mishnah to Symmachus in this way. When did Symmachus say that the division is made without an oath? Only in a case where there is actual loss of money involved. [*The phrase derara demamona means loss of money, since if the owner of the ox has to pay without cause, he suffers a real loss; and if he is acquitted unjustly then the owner of the dead calf unfairly loses the value of his animal.*] However, where there is no loss, as in our Mishnah, then Symmachus would rule for the imposition of an oath. But surely we should come to the opposite conclusion through the logical argument of *kal va' homer!*[17] If in the case of the gored animal where there is a certain loss for each one who may be in the right [*because whoever is in the right necessarily loses half the value of the calf when the liability is shared*]—since in fact it is only one or the other who is the sole rightful beneficiary [*by the nature of the case the owner of the calf is entitled to full damages, or the owner of the ox is completely free of responsibility*]—if there they share without an oath then how much more so should we rule the same in our Mishnah [*that they share without an oath*] where there is no loss of money for either of them. [*Moreover, one can even argue that they both took hold of the found article at the same time.*] However, we can still conclude that our Mishnah can be reconciled with Symmachus, and say that the oath imposed on the finders is a rabbinical law instituted to discourage anyone getting

hold [tokef, *to take hold*] of his fellow's garment claiming,
'It is mine.'

Based on several biblical verses in Exodus 21–2, the Talmud
lays down four main classes of damage for which a person is
legally responsible. The terms of these four classes of damage are:
'the ox' (which includes a man's animal or property as the
immediate damager), 'the pit' (public nuisance), 'the tooth'
(destruction of another's property) and 'the fire' (negligence as
the source of damage). These are explicitly mentioned in the
Bible and the owner of the animal or the negligent person is
liable to pay damages in full. These four classes of damages are
called in the Talmud *avoth nezikin*, literally 'fathers' or
'principles'. There are a number of other kinds of damage caused
by activities which are derived from the *avoth* and are known as
toledoth, literally 'offspring', or second category of damage. In
that case the responsible person pays half damages.

The Bible also rules that an animal which is a habitual
damager involves its owner in full damages. Such an animal is
called a *muad*. The Mishnah which follows categorizes the
damage caused by an animal in the normal course of its walking
as the damage of a *muad*. Such damage comes under the main
heading of the 'foot', which is a part of the first of the *avoth* listed
above. If some small stones are dislodged by the animal's walk
and they cause damage, such damage is a derivative of the 'foot'
and is categorized by the term 'pebbles'.

By following the Rashi of this Mishnah we are able to see
more clearly the several different cases of damages which are
found in the Mishnah. Most importantly, we can see why in
some situations there is full liability and in others there is only
half. Rashi's comments emphasize the difference between the
usual kind of damage, for which there is full responsibility, and
the damage caused in unusual circumstances. His comments in
this passage are a good illustration of his concern always to find
clear reasons for talmudic rulings.

The following is a list of the several damages in the first
category, with the reasons for full or half responsibility.

  1. Damages caused by the principle 'foot' are normal and

are expected with an animal in the course of its moving. Therefore the owner pays full damages.

2. Kicking is not usual and is a derivative of the 'horn' or goring. Therefore the man is liable only for half the damages.

3. 'Pebbles', though a normal occurence, is a derivative of 'foot'. Therefore, in spite of its being a usual occurrence, the owner of the animal pays only half damages. The fact that it is a usual source of damage seems to be outweighed by the fact that it is only a derivative source of damage. Rashi further supports the talmudic decision by adding the words that it 'is a law handed down by the rabbis'.

4. The animal trod on a utensil. This belongs clearly to the damages of the principle 'foot' and the owner of the animal pays in full.

5. Pieces of the broken vessel fall on a second utensil and break it. The case falls under the heading of 'pebbles' and the man pays half.

6. Any contraption tied to the feet of a fowl which causes damage to property, or the fowl hopping on a spot, making loose stones fly off and cause damage, fall under the category of 'pebbles'. Since it is a derivative source of damage the owner pays only half.

[MISHNAH, Baba Kama, 17a]   In what respect is the 'foot' like a habitual destroyer? [*i.e., In what way is the 'foot' like a confirmed source of damage?*] In that it breaks anything in its path in the course of moving. [*It is a confirmed habitual source of damage because even in the course of normal walking it breaks anything in its way.*] The animal is a regular destroyer [*the Gemara asks why the apparent duplication*] because as it moves it destroys anything in its path.

But if it kicked [*this is not normal and it is really a derivative of the 'horn', or goring. In this case he pays only half damages and no more*], or if some small stones flew off from under its feet and broke some vessels, then the owner of the animal pays half damages. [*Although this last case is not unusual—in fact it is quite usual—nevertheless he pays no more than half damages. This is the law as handed down by the rabbis.*

Furthermore he is liable only if the damage took place in the plaintiff's domain. This because 'pebbles' is only a derivative of 'foot' and there is no liability if damage under such circumstances took place in the public thoroughfare.]

If the animal trod on a vessel and broke it, and pieces fell on a vessel [*a second utensil*] and broke it, the owner of the animal has to pay full damages in connection with the first utensil, but only half damages for the second one. [*In the case of the first utensil the damage was caused by the 'foot' and so the man is fully liable. But the second utensil was damaged by 'pebbles' which is a derivative, and therefore he pays only half.*]

Cocks are considered regular destroyers when they break items in the course of their walking. If there was some contraption (Hebrew, *delil*) attached to its feet [*anything at all attached to its feet is called* delil. *Some versions substitute* deli (a bucket)] or if it was scratching [*the word means 'hopping'*] and some utensils were broken then the owner pays half damages. [*Because the case is just like damages through 'pebbles' since in the course of the fowl's hopping about some pebbles fell on the utensil and broke it.*]

Our next excerpt contains the rabbinic discussion on the law of *lex talionis*. According to the literal word of the Bible, a man who injures his fellow shall be punished by having the same injury inflicted upon him. So we read (Ex. 21:23–5), *Eye for eye, tooth for tooth, hand for hand, foot for foot, burning for burning, wound for wound, stripe for stripe.* (See also Lev. 24:19–20.) Now the rabbis never accepted this literally, but interpreted it to mean that the offender has to pay monetary compensation to the victim. The eighth chapter of the tractate begins with the Mishnah giving the details of the five headings under which the offender is liable. The Gemara enters into a long and close discussion on the rabbinic exegesis which allowed the rabbis to promulgate their non-literal and liberal interpretation.

Note that Rashi enters into the discussion only to clarify a point here and there. He is mostly content to stand aside and let the rabbinic discussion—where it seems clear enough—speak for itself.

[GEMARA, Baba Kama, 83 b ff.]   Why should the offender merely pay compensation? Surely the Bible explicitly says, *Eye for eye* etc. (Ex. 21:24)? So let us say then that it is to be taken literally. The answer is that we cannot accept such a meaning of the biblical rule. It has been taught: You might think that one who put out the eye of his fellow should have his own eye put out, or one who cut off another's hand should have his hand cut off, or one who broke another man's leg should have his own leg broken in retaliation; you should know that it is not so since the Bible says, *He that smiteth any man ... And he that smiteth a beast* (Lev. 24:17–18). [*Further on in the discussion the Gemara clarifies the matter by showing exactly which verses are involved in this exegesis.*] The verses are put together for comparison. Just as one who smites a beast has to pay compensation, so too one who smites another man has to pay compensation. If you wish [*if you find difficulty in accepting this reason, then the Gemara will now give you another reason*], you can argue as follows. The Bible lays down the law, *Ye shall take no ransom for the life of a murderer that is guilty of death* (Num. 35:31). That is to say, for the life of a *murderer* you can accept no payment as ransom, but you do take monetary compensation for an injury to limbs even if the injury is permanent. [*Since the eye, hand, foot etc. which the offender put out or broke cannot grow again, i.e. they 'do not come back'.*]

We have learned in a baraita R. Dostai b. Judah said: The law *eye for eye* laid down in Scripture means monetary compensation. That is what you say, but perhaps it is meant to be taken literally? That is impossible, for supposing the eye of one was large and the eye of the other was small, how is it possible to apply the strict letter of the law, *eye for eye*? And you cannot argue that only in such a case should the offender pay compensation since the Bible insists, *Ye shall have one manner of law* (Lev. 24:22), that is to say the same law for everyone. Now some rabbis refuted this argument. 'This is no question,' they said. 'If a man take away the sight of his fellow, then the Divine law lays down that his sight be taken away from him. And if you object to such a law on the basis of your previous argument what happens if a small man [*a dwarf*] kills a giant, or the opposite, how then can you put the murderer to death since the Torah rules *Ye shall have one manner of the law (ibid.)* that is to say, one equal law for all. The fact is that the murderer took a life, therefore the Divine law is that his life be taken away. So in the same way in our present case, the offender took away sight; and the Divine law is that his sight be taken away.'

The discussion continues in another baraita where, we read, R. Simeon bar Yochai said: *Eye for eye* means compensation. You say compensation, but perhaps it is intended to be applied literally? That is impossible, for supposing a blind man put out another man's eye or a man with one arm amputated another man's arm, how can we apply the strict law *eye for eye*, and the Torah rules *Ye shall have one manner of law. [We repeat part of the argument before this phrase, i.e., 'And should you say that only in that case we exact monetary compensation, the Torah rules that out in emphasizing that you shall have* one manner of law.] But this argument is refuted by holding that retaliation is carried out where it is possible, but where it is impossible then the offender goes free [*entirely. And under the circumstances it is still considered equal justice either to exact retaliation or to set him free if that is not possible*] because otherwise what will you do in the case of a dying man who murders a healthy man? There you can't punish the murderer. [*Since in the definition of the law he is already a 'dead' man. Such a one cannot be condemned by witnesses, since witnesses in such a case cannot be confuted. This is because confuted witnesses in such a case are acquitted since their evidence sought to condemn a man already 'dead'. Technically then, there are no witnesses, so the murderer is also acquitted. This is the law as explained in San. 78a.*][18] So we see, where it is possible to carry out the law, we do so; and where it is impossible, we send the offender free.

The School of Ishmael taught: Scripture says, *So shall it be rendered* (lit., 'given') *to him again* (Lev. 24:19). Now the word 'to give' can apply only to monetary compensation. Objection: Would the words *as he hath maimed* (lit., 'given a blemish to') *a man*[19] also refer to money? Surely not! The answer is that in the School of R. Ishmael this verse was expounded as superfluous, since the previous verse had already stated *And if a man maim* (give a blemish to) *his neighbour; as he hath done so shall it be done to him.* So why do we need a repetition of the law with the words, *so shall it be rendered* (given) *unto him?* It must therefore come to teach that it refers to monetary compensation...

The School of Hiyya taught: Scripture says, *hand for* (lit., 'in') *hand.*[20] [*This verse also speaks about an* ed zomem, *a false witness who has been confuted. If such a person testified against another man that he had cut off the hand of his fellow, and he was found to be an* ed zomem, *then he, the 'witness', has to pay monetary compensation.*] This implies something that is given from hand to hand. What is that? Money.

Let us turn to representative examples of another kind, from the vast storehouse of rabbinic folklore which punctuates the Talmud in numerous places. Here we are not dealing with the dialectic of rabbinic debate, or subtle points of legalistic argument. Instead, the rabbis are telling a story: usually a very good story. But we have to face an immediate question. Is the story historical, or is it a parable through which the rabbis wished to submit a lesson? We cannot enter into this problem here, but we can point out that where most modern students of the Talmud will try to examine the story as a legend or as a parable with a worthwhile rabbinic moral, the medieval teachers would probably see it as the record of something which actually happened, and would therefore not be interested in even asking the question, 'What is the point of this story?' As we have already indicated in a different context, Rashi is a representative of the eleventh-century mind, living in a milieu which is far removed from philosophical, historical, or theological analysis. He is the transmitter of the Jewish heritage, not its critic. It is fairly safe to asssume that in the following few representative pieces of folklore, Rashi sees the account as a reported tradition of an event which actually happened. He asks no questions about it, and is not concerned with the philosophical or theological implications. That is why there is a noticeable absence of any real atttempt to explain the story, except of course to give the *peshat* or plain meaning of difficult words and phrases.

The following story is justly famous for the many insights which it provides into the rabbinic concept of Torah, particularly of Torah as a supreme value which develops from age to age. But Rashi ignores all this rich source of rabbinic theology.

[GEMARA, Menahoth, 29b]   Rabbi Judah said in the name of Rab: When Moses went up to God he found God sitting and putting little crowns [*decorative crownlets on several letters of the Torah*] on the letters. Moses asked, 'Why do You have to do this?' [*Why do You have to add these crowns to what You have already written?*] God replied, 'Because a man is to appear on earth after many generations. Akiba ben Joseph is his name, and from the tip of each of these letters of the Torah he will expound heaps and heaps of rulings.' Moses said, 'Show him to me.' So God replied, 'Turn around.' Moses did so, and he went and sat down at the end of the eighth row of Akiba's students. But when he realized that he did not understand a single thing of what was being said, he felt faint. Then when Akiba came to a certain matter [*which needed an explanation*] his disciples asked him how he knew that, and Akiba replied, 'This is a teaching delivered to Moses on Mount Sinai.' Then his mind was put at rest. [*The mind of Moses. Although Moses himself did not receive Akiba's later teaching, he was now reconciled to the situation because Akiba named him as his source.*]

Although our next tale is still within the framework of the

rabbinic concept of Torah and its importance, it would seem from the end of the story that even Torah knowledge is not as important as altruistic love. Again, it is noticeable that Rashi deals only with the *peshat* and not with the ideas.

[GEMARA, Ketuboth, 77b]   Rabbi Johanan made an announcement: Beware of the flies which have touched sufferers of raatan.[21] [*Flies which land on the sick person can transmit the disease to someone else.*] R. Zeira never sat in the same atmosphere. [*In a place where the same wind would blow over them both.*] R. Eleazar would never enter a sufferer's tent. R. Ami and R. Assi even avoided eating eggs bought in the street where the sick person lived. However, R. Joshua b. Levi associated [*sat together with them to study Torah and believed that the Torah would protect him so that he would not be harmed*] with such persons and studied Torah with them. Quoting the verse, *A lovely hind and a graceful doe*[22] he said: If the Torah bestows grace on those who study it, will it not also protect them? When he was about to die [*when his time came to die*[23]] the angel of death was instructed to carry out his wishes. When the angel came and appeared before the rabbi, Joshua ben Levi said, 'Show me my place.' [*i.e., 'Take me to Paradise and show me my place there.'*] The angel agreed. The rabbi added another request, 'Now hand over your sword in case you frighten me on our way.' The angel handed over his sword. When they arrived at the other place, the angel lifted up the rabbi and showed him what was there, whereupon Rabbi Joshua jumped down (the translation of the Aramaic verb here is Rashi's—'to jump') and landed on the other side. The angel grabbed hold of the edges of the rabbi's coat [*to pull him back*] but Joshua said, 'I swear that I will not return.' Then God said, 'If he has ever had an oath annulled in his life [*if he has ever made an oath which he then sought the authorities to annul. The word 'itshall' from the Hebrew 'shaal'*] then he must return; but if not, then he need not return.' The angel then said, 'Give me back my sword.' But Rabbi Joshua refused. So a heavenly voice was heard: 'Give it back because he needs it for his work with mortal man.'

The prophet Elijah announced the rabbi's arrival, 'Make way for the son of Levi! Make way for the son of Levi!' Rabbi Joshua entered and he saw Rabbi Simeon bar Yochai sitting on thirteen stools of gold. (Rashi here gives the meaning of the Aramaic word 'takteki' in a *laaz* meaning 'stools'.) 'Are you the son of Levi?' he asked. 'I am,' answered Joshua. 'Did a rainbow ever appear in your lifetime?' asked R. Simeon. 'Yes,' answered Joshua. 'In that case you can't be the son of Levi,' said Simeon. [*You don't deserve the reputation; because the rainbow is only a reminder of the Covenant God made that He would not destroy the world, but in a generation where there is a perfectly righteous man then such a sign is not needed.*] In fact no rainbow was seen in Joshua's lifetime; but he answered as he did thinking, 'I do not wish to take any credit for myself.'

R. Hanina ben Papa was his friend [*of the angel of death who would visit him*[24]], and when his time came to die the angel was instructed to carry out his wishes... When the angel appeared the rabbi said, 'Show me my place,' and the angel agreed. 'Now give me your sword,' requested Hanina, 'in case you frighten me on the way.' At this, the angel called out, 'Do you want to do to me what your colleague tried to do?' Hanina answered, 'Bring me a Torah and you will see that there is not a single thing in it which I have failed to obey.' Whereupon the angel of death challenged him, 'But have you ever sat down with sufferers of raatan [*like Joshua ben Levi, who risked his life for the honour of Torah*] and studied Torah with them?'

We will take one more example from talmudic *aggadah*. Again the legend is well known, not only because the story is a good one but because it is one with a profound meaning and deals with a central concept in Jewish theology.

[GEMARA, Sanhedrin, 98a]   Rabbi Joshua ben Levi asked Elijah the prophet, 'When will the Messiah come?'

The prophet replied, 'Go and ask him yourself.'

'Where is he to be found?' asked the rabbi.

'At the gates of the city,' answered Elijah. [*My teacher thought that what is meant is not the actual city* (Rome) *gates. The whole world is paralleled in Paradise. And what Elijah said was that in that spot in Paradise which is opposite the gates of the city, you will find the Messiah.*]

'And how will I recognize him?' the rabbi wanted to know.

'He is sitting among the poor and the diseased,' said Elijah. [*They are covered in sores. The Messiah is also wounded, as it is written,* For he was wounded because of our transgressions (Isa 53 : 5), *and it is written,* Our diseases he did bear (verse 4).] All of them untie all the bandages and bind all the sores. [*All those with several sores untie and bind them all in one operation. They remove the entire bandage, clean the wounds and rebind them all.*] Whereas he unties the bandages of each sore [*He, the Messiah, removes the bandage of one sore, cleanses the wound and rebinds it. Then he goes on to treat the next one in the same way. He would not treat two wounds together, thinking that if he were suddenly called to proceed on his mission to redeem Israel, he would not want to be delayed even by the time it takes to tie up two wounds*] separately, thinking that should he be called to come he would not be delayed.

So Rabbi Joshua went there and greeted the Messiah, 'Peace be to you my master and teacher.'

'Peace to you O son of Levi,' answered the Messiah.

'When will the master come?'

'Today.' [*Rabbi Joshua to Messiah: 'When will the master come?' He answered, 'Today.'*]

The rabbi then returned to Elijah the prophet who asked him, 'What did the Messiah say to you?'

'He simply said, "Peace to you O son of Levi,"' he reported.

'That means,' said Elijah, 'he promised you and your father a share in the world to come.' [*For if you were not perfectly righteous he would not have greeted you as he did or remembered your father's name.*]

'But he lied to me,' protested the rabbi, 'because he said, "I will come today": but he did not come.'

To this the prophet replied, 'This is what he meant, *Today, if ye would but hearken to His voice*' (Ps. 95:7). [*The voice of God.*]

These few examples of talmudic folklore demonstrate the clear difference between Rashi's commentaries on the halachic or legalistic sections of the Talmud and his treatment of the *aggadah*. In the former he is the total exponent of rabbinic method, the eternal guide for all the talmudic principles of interpretation and the master of talmudic language. With these tools he guides the reader through the most difficult passages of legalistic argumentation and removes all obstacles to an understanding of the text. In the *aggadah* of the Talmud he explains only the text and not the ideas or the principles. This is not to denigrate Rashi's Talmud commentaries. Perhaps the reverse is true. For the halachic or legal sections generally lead to a conclusion which must ultimately be reflected in the law. The ideas of the *aggadah*, however, remain wide open to many different interpretations. All Rashi attempts here is to make the story clear. Its meaning can then be independently pursued—undoubtedly with a variety of different conclusions.

5

RASHI'S LASTING INFLUENCE

I

The literary eminence of a nation is frequently upheld by a few immortal classics. Thus, English literature is permanently enriched by a Chaucer, a Shakespeare or a Milton—even as their works enriched the entire world. Further back in history, the writings of Plato and Aristotle are monuments which marked ancient Greece as the cradle of philosophical thought and which exercised a lasting influence on the development of ideas in every civilized country. And the same thing can be said of any nation which has one or two books which are precious to it, from which it educates itself and from which the rest of the world can draw inspiration.[1]

For the Jewish people, setting aside the Bible and the Talmud, such a book is Rashi's commentary on the Bible. While his commentary on the Talmud performs a vital function for the very large proportion of the Jewish people who are Talmud students, it is the commentary on the Bible, and particularly the commentary on the Humash (Pentateuch) which had and still has the much wider influence. Any Jew who studied the Humash with Rashi—and this was basic curriculum even in the elementary Hebrew school—was no longer an ignoramus but was involved with the Torah and its spirit from the early years of his life. By any standard of evaluation Rashi's commentaries have had the most profound influence on Jewish life and letters and it would be difficult to point to any single post-talmudic work which has had such an influence. This is not to detract from the importance of, say, Maimonides (twelfth century) or Joseph Caro (sixteenth century). Indeed, the works of both those master Jewish thinkers, as of others, are truly monumental and contributed enormously to the direction of Judaism and to the character of the Jewish people. But the fact remains that those works were closely followed by the scholars rather than by the broad masses. In this respect, Rashi's commentaries had a much wider appeal and their influence went far beyond the restricted circles of the scholars. Rashi's work went out to the people. Among many students who read the Ḥumash with Rashi in their childhood, the words of Rashi occasionally became indistinguishable from the biblical text itself, so that sometimes they did not know what they were quoting, the Ḥumash or Rashi.[2]

It may be that when Rashi wrote his Talmud commentary he had in mind not so much an audience of laymen but a smaller and select group of serious students.[3] But with his Bible commentary he certainly took account of the fact that his work would be used by the wider public. And even with respect to the Talmud commentary, whoever may have been Rashi's original intended reading public, the fact remains that in the course of time, and particularly after the introduction of printing, more and more people studied the Talmud, and with it Rashi's commentary became the undisputed and indispensable guide.

II

Rashi's influence on subsequent Jewish scholarship came quickly and proved lasting. His first circle of influence was his own family who were also his disciples. In his family he was most fortunate because from the very start his work spread through them, his reputation was more easily established, the schools of rabbinic scholarship in northern France were strengthened and new ones were established.

Judah ben Nathan, the husband of Rashi's daughter Miriam, was a distinguished talmudist who, as noted above, completed some of Rashi's commentaries on the Talmud.[4] His other son-in-law, Meir ben Samuel of Rameru, maintained an important rabbinic centre in his home town. In addition to heading the school there he also wrote Responsa under the guidance of his distinguished father-in-law. Meir and Rashi's younger daughter Jochabed had four sons and a daughter. Each son became an outstanding scholar, rabbinic authority and author in his own right. The most famous of them were Samuel (Rashbam) and Jacob, who was known as Rabbenu Tam, after the verse in Genesis 25:27 where Jacob the patriarch is described as *tam*, a man of integrity. The other two sons were Solomon and Isaac.

Samuel ben Meir studied under his grandfather Rashi and apparently succeeded him as head of the academy in Troyes. But Samuel was of a strong, independent spirit, and he established in Rameru, his own father's birthplace, a new academy which became one of the rabbinic schools of great importance in the period following Rashi's death. It was in Rameru that Samuel wrote his valuable commentary on the Bible which, after Rashi, is the gem of French Bible exegesis. The great feature of Rashbam's commentary is its emphasis on *peshat*. In this respect he was more consistent than his illustrious grandfather, and he resolutely rejected midrashic methods of interpretation when it came to the Bible text.

Another French Bible exegete of great importance was Joseph ben Simeon Kara (born about 1060), one of Rashi's nephews. He enjoyed collaboration with his uncle who encouraged him in his work of Bible interpretation. Some of Kara's insights are in fact incorporated into Rashi's commentary. Kara is also quoted by Rashbam, who calls him 'our colleague'.[5]

In the world of Jewish scholarship numerous commentaries on the Bible were produced within a few centuries after Rashi. In time what one can call a 'short list' of top commentators grew up through a process of selection by serious students and perceptive teachers. The Rabbinic Bible, known as *Mikraot Gedolot*, publishes over forty such commentaries, in abbreviated form and covering only selected books of the Bible. Among the most outstanding of them are the following: Rashbam (1085–1174), Abraham ibn Ezra (1089–1164), Radak (David Kimhi, 1160–1235), Ramban (Moses ben Nahman, known as Nahmanides, (1194–1270), and Isaac Abrabanel (1437–1509). Each of these is a Bible commentator of great importance in his own right, yet, outshining them all by far, Rashi takes pride of place and his commentary is usually printed immediately next to the Bible text itself. In fact it is a mark of Rashi's impact on Jewish life and thought that priority was given to Rashi after the introduction of printing: the very first Hebrew book to be printed was Rashi's commentary on the Pentateuch—without the Pentateuch itself. It was published in Reggio, Italy, in February 1475 and in Spain the following year. The Pentateuch itself was not printed until 1482—together with Rashi's commentary. The 'Rashi script' in which the commentary is usually printed is really just the printer's type. The first edition of Rashi in 1475 appeared in this form and therefore became known as 'Rashi script'. It is assumed that the printer devised this type because it was space saving. Subsequently it was used for printing all rabbinic commentaries. Among other advantages it clearly distinguished the text from the commentary.

Rashbam's younger brother Jacob was a small child when his grandfather died, but he grew up to become one of the most outstanding scholars of the twelfth century. He wrote many Responsa—his opinions were sought by scholars all over Europe—and was also a noted exegete and grammarian. In addition, he wrote poetry and liturgical pieces. His life was unfortunately saddened by the cruelties of the Crusades in which several of his friends and colleagues lost their lives. He tells us how on the second day of Shavuoth he himself was robbed and wounded by a marauding gang of crusader soldiers, and was only saved from death by the intervention of the neighbouring baron.

There is a curious and interesting tradition with regard to Rashi, his grandson Jacob and the *mezuzah* which is fixed on the doors of the Jewish home.[6] According to Rashi, the *mezuzah* should be fixed in a vertical position. Years later however, Jacob ruled that it should lie horizontally on the doorpost. So in deference to the opinions of the noted grandfather and his eminent grandson the custom of fixing the *mezuzah* in a diagonal position developed.

Within the same framework of ritualistic laws and customs there was a debate about the order of the four biblical passages inserted in the *tephillin*.[7] Rashi, Maimonides and other rabbinic authorities ruled that the order of the passages should be in accordance with their biblical sequence: Ex. 13:1–10; 11–16; Deut. 6:4–9; 11:13–21. Rabbenu Tam, however, was of the opinion that the order of the two paragraphs in Deuteronomy should be reversed.[8] Such was the recognized authority of Rabbenu Tam, that many Jews to this very day put on two pairs of *tephillin*, the first with the paragraphs in the generally accepted order, and the second pair, called Rabbenu Tam's *tephillin*, worn for the conclusion of the service.

Rabbenu Tam was one of the first of the school of tosaphists, who set out to supplement the commentary of Rashi on the Talmud. Hence their work is rightly called Tosaphoth, i.e. additional comments. Unlike Rashi, the tosaphists did not compile a running commentary on the Talmud text, but take up a point here and there which calls for more analytical examination. They raise questions and offer criticisms, always with a view to bringing clarity and consistency to the talmudic argument. In very many cases they took Rashi as the starting point of their own examination, but, while they showed great veneration for 'The Commentary' (of Rashi), they were never bashful in criticizing or suggesting corrections to the master's interpretations.

Isaac ben Samuel was another leading tosaphist and a descendant of Rashi. Known as Isaac the Elder, he led the academy at Rameru for a time, but later founded a school of his own at Dampierre. There he is said to have had sixty students, each of whom knew a complete tractate of the Talmud by heart.

The list of distinguished scholars of the tosaphist school grew, as did the number of schools in France. Important schools were also founded outside Champagne, and at this time Paris became an important centre of Talmud study. The outstanding tosaphist of the Paris school was Judah ben Isaac (also called Gur Aryeh, 1166–1224), also a descendant of Rashi. Among the most distinguished of his many pupils was Moses ben Jacob of Coucy, the author of a very important book on Jewish law called *Sefer Mitzvoth Gadol* (abbreviated to SeMaG) which was influenced by the great code of Maimonides and the decisions of the French tosaphists.

III

Rashi's influence was accepted in northern Europe during the scholar's lifetime, since his work was immediately known, and all his successors, even those who disagreed with him, leaned on him. Within a century after Rashi's death his fame had spread to other countries. In spite of some strong criticism of his extensive use of *derush*, the Spanish Jewish scholar and Bible commentator Abraham ibn Ezra (1089–1164) wrote a poem praising Rashi. Spanish scholars in general were critical of their peers in France, but Rashi was the exception. Based on ibn Ezra's poem, called *Parshandata* (Bible Interpreter), there arose the humorous line prevalent in Spanish circles, *Kol perushe Tzarfarta holech le-ashpata, hutz mi-Parshdata!* (All the interpretations of the French are fit to be thrown away—with the exception of those of the Parshandata, i.e. Rashi). Admiration of Rashi's work was also expressed years later, by Maimonides (1135–1204) and Nahmanides (1194–1270).

In 1200, Abraham Zutra of Thebes became the first of a long line of scholars who wrote a series of super-commentaries on Rashi's Bible commentary. The fact that numerous such super-commentaries were written in the course of time is substantial evidence of the influence of Rashi's work and the central place it held in the world of Jewish scholarship. Scholars have found over a hundred super-commentaries in complete or partial form, in print or in manuscript.[9] Some of those writings were composed by well-known scholars. The most important was by Elijah Mizrahi (sixteenth century), the outstanding rabbinic authority of his time. He examines almost every word in Rashi's commentary, defending the master against criticism, particularly that of Nahmanides, although he does not hesitate to disagree with Rashi whenever he sees fit to do so. Rashi's commentary together with Mizrahi's super-commentary were staple texts for rabbinic students after the sixteenth century. But the most popular of all the super-commentaries on Rashi was the *Sifte Hachamim* on the Pentateuch by Shabbetai Bass (1680). This is generally the only major super-commentary printed today in the standard edition of the *Mikraot Gedolot*, the Rabbinic Bible. This is not due to the fact that, among other accomplishments, Bass himself was a printer, but to the more relevant fact that his super-commentary is intrinsically interesting and valuable. The author generally assumes that a Rashi comment on the text is motivated by some textual difficulty—Rashi would not presume to make an unnecessary comment. The average reader is often unaware of the hidden question which concerned Rashi. In revealing the question, Bass frequently casts light on the master's interpretation.

Rashi's successors in the field of talmudic commentary also acknowledged their indebtedness to him. Simon ben Zemah Duran (fourteenth century), himself a commentator and rabbinic authority, wrote in the course of his own work on a talmudic treatise, 'We have placed before us the commentary of Rabbi Solomon of blessed memory who is unmatched in explaining statements according to the intention of their authors.'[10]

Rashi's commentary appears in every edition of the Talmud. Other commentaries are found only in the standard Vilna edition (1880) and in its facsimile editions. The Tosaphoth, the additional commentaries compiled by Rashi's descendants and successors in northern France and surrounding countries are next in importance. Because of their close relationship with the Rashi commentary they also appear in virtually every edition of the Talmud, and are positioned on the opposite side of the page to Rashi's commentary. From what must have been a veritable mass of early and later commentaries the Vilna edition prints the following: Rabbi Hananel (990–1050), Rabbenu Gershom of Mainz (960–1028), and Rabbi Nissim, a pupil of Rabbi Hananel. Among the post-Rashi commentaries we find the *Torah Or* and *Ein Mishpat* by Joseph Boaz (sixteenth century) and the *Masoreth Hashass* by Isaiah Berlin (1725–99). Those three works are cross-references to Bible quotations in the Talmud texts, legal rulings codified in later authoritative code books based on the talmudic discussion, and parallel texts in other places in the

Talmud, in that order. In addition there are the suggested alternative readings for both the Talmud text and the Rashi commentary by Joel Sirkes (sixteenth century) called *Hagahot Ha-Bah*. In the same class of marginal annotations there are the *Hagahot Ha-Gra* of Elijah of Vilna (1720–97) and the glosses of Akiva Eger (1761–1837), whose annotations, critical and explanatory notes are listed under a compilation known as *Gilyon Ha-Shass*.

But as we have seen in the case of the Bible commentaries, so too with the Talmud commentaries. Many of them take up a point raised by Rashi, either in agreement or disagreement. Again, pride of place is given to Rashi's commentary: hardly an edition fails to print it—even the least expensive paperback of a single treatise will include the Rashi commentary.[11]

So impressive is Rashi's influence that several writers consider that the master commentator wrote with the power of Divine inspiration. Of course something like this can be said of all creative writers: it is a way of describing the gift we call genius. But in the case of Rashi it meant rather the direct communication of the Divine spirit to the great teacher. Isaiah Horowitz (1565–1630), the great Polish rabbi and leader, observed, 'Everything which Rashi wrote contains the most wonderful insights, for his work was written with Divine inspiration.' Rashi himself might have been conscious of something like this when he notes on Ezekiel 42:3: 'I had neither instructor nor assistance in this work—only help from God.'

From what has so far been said, the impression might be given that Rashi's influence was confined to works of medieval scholarship. This is far from the truth. Modern Jewish scholarship is also heavily indebted to the eleventh-century teacher and relies significantly on his insights. The three outstanding and popular Bible commentaries in English for the Jewish reader are the *Hertz Pentateuch*,[12] the *Soncino Bible*,[13] and *The Torah*, recently published under the auspices of the American Reform Movement.[14] Even a casual survey of these popular works will indicate the influence of Rashi on modern works of Jewish Bible commentary.[15]

A similar statement can be made about Rashi's influence on modern Talmud commentary, where his influence can be said to be even stronger. No modern student in any academy will omit reading the Rashi: the Talmud text and the Rashi commentary invariably go together. The most successful modern commentary on the Talmud is the Steinsaltz Talmud,[16] which is today very widely used by students who find its numerous modern features helpful and appealing. Its greatest contribution is a running commentary in simple modern Hebrew in the style of the Rashi running commentary on the Talmud. A similar attempt with English commentaries was made with a publication titled *Talmud El Am*.[17] In both cases the editors rely very significantly on Rashi. The Steinsaltz Talmud publishes the Rashi text in full, in its usual place on the inside margin. The *El Am* does not print the Rashi text, but it is abundantly clear that the commentary is heavily dependent on Rashi's interpretations.

IV

From the thirteenth century a new style of biblical commentary became evident. Most of the later commentators on the Bible departed from the earlier emphasis on the *peshat*—in fact they seemed to go to the other extreme. Not only did they introduce a great deal of *aggadah* into their commentaries, but they also indulged in *gematria*, the 'science' of the significance of numbers, and the kind of mystical interpretation which had been so resolutely rejected by Rashi, by Rashbam and their schools. This is not to say that the importance of Rashi's commentary diminished; but in this period the spirit of rational interpretation, with close regard to the actual meaning of the text, waned in popularity. The pride of place of Rashi's name and work was still respected, but the methodological emphasis had now shifted from *peshat* to *derush* and even to mysticism. It is more than probable that the increasing insecurity of Jewish life at this time created a mood where mystical and non-rational interpretations of the Bible text were more acceptable.

At about the same time Christian exegesis was showing signs of moving in exactly the opposite direction. Chief among the new school of Christian scholars and exegetes was a Franciscan monk, Nicholas de Lyra (*c.* 1270–1340). In addition to his aim of freeing Christian exegesis from the suffocating effects of mysticism, he had one clear technical advantage over all his colleagues—his superb knowledge of Hebrew: it was even thought that he must be a converted Jew. At all events, his fluency with Hebrew texts gave him the unique opportunity to study Rashi's commentary on the Bible. And not only did he study it; he absorbed it and relied very heavily on it. In a statement on his method of biblical commentary, Nicholas wrote, 'Proposing therefore to avoid these and similar practices (i.e., the folkloristic and mystical expositions) I intend to insist on the literal meaning, and to insert occasionally a very few brief mystical interpretations; although seldom.' This is a clear paraphrase of Rashi's own declaration of intent found in his comment on Genesis 3:8. Nicholas de Lyra also postulated the twin methods of interpretation which he called the *sensus literalis* and the *sensus mysticus*. As we have seen he follows Rashi's intention to keep close to the literal sense. He goes on to declare, 'In like manner I intend for making the literal sense, to introduce not only the statements of the Catholic doctors, but also of the Hebrews, especially Rabbi Salomon, who among the Hebrew doctors has spoken most reasonably.' The Christian interpreter frequently introduces a comment by acknowledging Rashi as his source, saying *Rabbi Salomon hoc posit*. As for his commentary on the Psalms, it is frequently seen as a paraphrase of Rashi. So much is he indebted to the Jewish scholar that uncharitable critics called him *Simia Salomonis*, Rashi's Ape. Nicholas de Lyra's influence on Christian scholarship was enormous. In his Bible translation, Martin Luther relied very heavily on his expository work, a line of influence which was humorously emphasized by the quip, *Si Lyra non lyrasset Lutherius non saltasset*, which is to say, 'If Lyra had not played, Luther could not have danced.' Thus we see that the great movement of Bible translations was significantly influenced by the work of Rashi, through Nicholas and continuing with Luther and the Reformation scholars, for whom a mastery of the Scriptures was of central importance.

V

The intense period of Bible and Talmud studies continued to at least the end of the thirteenth century. By that time the political insecurity of French Jewry and the disastrous effects of the Crusades had brought about a decline of the schools and the exodus of their students to other lands. In 1239 an apostate, Nicholas Donin, denounced the Talmud as anti-Christian, and Pope Gregory IX ordered all copies to be seized and an inquiry established. As a result, the Talmud was condemned and twenty-four cartloads of precious Hebrew Talmud and other manuscripts were publicly burned in Paris. This happened in 1242—two hundred and two years after Rashi's birth.

From that point onwards French Jewry suffered a period of decline. It is true that even after the book-burning of 1242, French Jewry continued to live in that country and to maintain its religious and intellectual life. But now it was in a much weaker position. One exile followed another, in 1306 and in 1360: and after each partial exile conditions grew worse. The Jews in France lived under the shadows of the blood libel, of mob riots and of accusations of desecrating the Christian Host. Clerical fanaticism lost few chances to stir up the maximum trouble for the saddened Jewish community. The final curtain fell on French medieval Jewry with the expulsion of all Jews from France in 1394, by the edict of Charles VI. The earlier period of tolerance and even brotherhood which had provided the congenial background for creative Jewish scholarship came to an end. But those centuries of fruitful activity were not lost: they left a glorious heritage of scholarship and spirituality which enriched Jewish life in the centuries which followed and which has informed Jewish life the world over to this very day.

NOTES

Translations from the works of Rashi and from the Talmud, unless othewise stated, are the author's. Biblical quotations are from the Jewish Publication Society translation, 1946. Full bibliographical information will be found in the Select Bibliography, pp. 108–9.

2: The Life of Rashi

1. Rashi refers explicitly to his father in his commentary on Avodah Zarah 75a, where he remarks, '... This is what my father of blessed memory said, and it appeals to me.' From this it might seem that Isaac was a learned man and possibly that he did not die in Rashi's childhood.
2. Legend records that Simeon's son Elhanan was kidnapped as an infant and baptized. He became a priest, then a cardinal and finally a pope. He returned to Judaism when he recognized his father after many years.
3. Liber, *Rashi*, p. 77.
4. *Ibid.*
5. Quoted by I. Agus in *Urban Civilization*, Yeshiva University, New York, 1965, p. 750.
6. Liber, op. cit., p. 79; cf. Rashi on Ezek. 26:1.
7. A comprehensive list of places where Rashi acknowledges lack of knowledge is found in Maimon, *Midei Hodesh Behodsho*, vol. 1, p. 788 ff.
8. See Rashbam, Commentary on Gen. 37:2.
9. Rashi, Commentary on Betzah, 2b.
10. Elfenbein, *Teshuvot Rashi*, p. 209, para. 180.
11. *Ibid.*, p. 179, para. 155.
12. Mishnah, Avodah Zarah, I,6.
13. Liber, op. cit., pp. 161–2.
14. *Ibid.*, p. 164.
15. Rashi, Commentary on Gen. 11:9.
16. Rashi, Commentary on Lev. 26:6.

3:   *The Bible Commentary*

1   Tosephta Sanhedrin VII,11.
2   Sifra.
3   Additions to tractate Berachoth.
4   End of tractate Berachoth.
5   Shabbath 63a.
6   We have already noted some of Rashi's polemical interpretation in Chapter 1. Other Rashi texts of the same kind are his comments on Pss. 2:12; 9:1; 38:1; 39:2–5; Prov. 14:10.
7   This aspect of scribal work was greatly extended in later years.
8   Tractate Soferim, a minor and late tractate of the Talmud. The first nine chapters deal with the laws of writing the sacred scrolls as well as with many laws connected with their correct reading.
9   See Liber, *Rashi*, p. 91.
10 See Commentary on I Chr. 29:11, where the commentator notes: 'This was explained to me by Rabbi Eliezer ben Meir.' This Rabbi Eliezer was a Bible scholar who lived in the twelfth century. Some scholars question Rashi's authorship of the entire commentary on the book of Job. Similar doubt has been cast on the commentaries on Ezra and Nehemiah.
11 I am indebted to Neeman, *Rashi Mefaresh Hatorah*, where several of these examples are noted.
12 It may be that the term is not so much a mnemonic, but a noun in its own right. *Loez* means a 'foreign people' as in Ps. 114:1.
13 Berliner, *Kuntrus Ha-Loazim*, is the most comprehensive. Another pioneering work is in French, Darmsteter, *Les Glosses Françaises de Raschi*.
14 Rashi on Gen. 37:35; 4:1; 6:3, 13; Num. 14:14.
15 Rashi on Ex. 12:5.
16 Rashi on Ex. 23:5; 34:9; Num. 9:13.
17 Rashi on Num. 9:15.
18 The date and the origins of the *teamim* and accent points is a moot question. The Talmud contains some early references to them, although at that time there was no formal system of punctuation or accents. Most studies indicate that as a full system the *teamim* owe their origin to the masoretes, a scholarly group of scribes, based in Tiberias, who were responsible for the careful preservation and transmission of the authentic text of the Bible. They flourished from the sixth to the ninth centuries.
19 Rashi on Gen. 29:6.
20 Rashi on Num. 19:7; 27:2. The liberalism of Rashi is more apparent than real since he had a classic precedent in the exegesis of Rabbi Eliezer who laid down thirty-two principles for biblical

interpretation. The thirty-first principle relates to the re-arrangement of words in the verse as a legitimate way of interpreting a biblical text. Even so, Rashi appears to show a reluctance in employing this method of interpretation except when there seems to be no other way to understand the text.

21 It has been suggested that Rashi's insistence on *peshat* as the first and most important meaning of the text was also motivated by his polemic with the Church where the plain meaning was twisted by mystical references to Christian dogma. See Neeman, op. cit., p. 17.

22 Liber, op. cit., p. 207. Quoted by Berliner, in his Introduction. In spite of this, ibn Ezra is credited with the authorship of a highly laudatory poem in praise of Rashi, the great *Parshandata* (Bible Interpreter).

23 The Abraham ibn Daud referred to here is not the same as the author of the famous *Sefer Ha-Kabbalah*. The manuscript containing the severe criticism of Rashi is No. 35 in Medieval Hebrew Manuscripts in the University Library, Cambridge, England.

24 Rashi's comment on Deut. 33:7 also offers the thought that Simeon's blessing is alluded to in Judah's blessing.

25 Rashbam commentary on Gen. 37:2.

26 In Bereshith Rabbah, R. Isaac is not mentioned as the source. J. L. Maimon quotes the seventeenth-century scholar David ben Samuel, who suggested that the Isaac referred to here is none other than Rashi's own father whom the great commentator honoured at the very beginning of his work by crediting a question to him. See Maimon, vol. I, p. 76.

27 Rashi's concern that a teacher shall do his work with total dedication is also noted in his comment on Talmud, Eruvin 54b, 'When a man teaches his disciple he is bound to give him the reason for everything he teaches—as far as he can. He should not tell his student, "This have I heard. Now you try to understand the meaning as best you can."' Note here also Rashi's emphasis on teaching the reason, the *ta'am* of the laws. The word is in fact a key term in Rashi's method.

4: *The Talmud Commentary*

1 Succah, 40a.

2 Temurah, 15b; Chullin, 81a.

3 Eduyoth, Middoth and Tamid (partial). The printed commentaries were written by other scholars.

4 There are some twelve treatises about which there is a scholarly debate whether the commentary is wholly or partially Rashi's. A list of these volumes is given by Liber, *Rashi*, pp. 232–3.

5 He thought, for example, that the River Euphrates flows from

Palestine into Babylon; or that the Nile overflows its banks once in forty years.

6 Quoted by Esra Shereshevsky in *Rashi, The Man and his World*, in the name of S. M. Chones, *Toledot Haposkim*, Warsaw, 1910, p. 7a.

7 Deut. 6:7; 11:19.

8 The portion of produce which was given as a gift to the priests. The food was holy and could be eaten by the priest and his family only in a state of purity.

9 Apparently in France, Germany and in other parts of Europe, during the summer months, it was the practice to read the Evening Service, including the Shema, several hours before dark. This in contravention of talmudic law. It is assumed that this was because in the long evenings of the summer it was unreasonable to expect the people to return for a third time to the synagogue for evening prayers. See Louis Jacobs, *A Tree of Life*, Oxford University Press, 1984, pp. 122 ff.

10 A tannaitic teaching which was not included in the official Mishnah of Judah the Prince.

11 Lev. 7:15.

12 A tanna is a teacher of the Mishnah who flourished, generally, any time before the codification of the Mishnah in 200 CE.

13 Deut. 6:7.

14 Gen. 1:5.

15 Such brief comments are typical of Rashi's style when he explains the Mishnah. He knows and anticipates his students' questions, and to avoid any unnecessary duplication of commentary seems to say, 'Have patience and all will be explained in good time.'

16 Deut. 19:21. The subject is the law of the return of lost property.

17 *kal va'homer*: from minor premise to major premise.

18 Until 1520 there was no pagination in the Talmud. So obviously Rashi himself does not give any cross references to a particular page of the Talmud. Instead, he refers the student to the tractate and to the chapter in that tractate which is identified by its first words. The first edition of the Talmud with an ordered pagination was printed by Daniel Bomberg, a Christian, who published all the tractates of the Talmud between 1520 and 1523. Subsequent editions of the printed Talmud followed Bomberg's edition together with its standard layout and pagination.

19 Lev. 24:20.

20 Deut. 19:21.

21 Raatan: a highly infectious and fatal disease.

22 Prov. 5:19. The verse is interpreted by the rabbis as applying to the Torah.

23 The language of Rashi suggests that R. Joshua died from natural causes, not from the infection to which he had exposed himself.

24 The normal translation is that Hanina was a friend of Joshua ben Levi, and this makes sense from the story as it develops. Rashi's gloss, however, makes Hanina the friend of the angel of death with whom he seems to have been on speaking terms. The text itself permits such a reading; but it is still rather odd. However, Rashi's explanation may be supported by the fact that Hanina lived at the end of the third and the beginning of the fourth centuries, while Joshua ben Levi lived in the first half of the third century. The two may therefore have never met. (Historical inaccuracies abound in the Talmud.) Rashi was acquainted with the line of the sages—tannaim and amoraim—and roughly when they lived. He might have thought, therefore, that his explanation was more accurate.

5: *Rashi's Lasting Influence*

1 Cf. *Iggrot C. N. Bialik* (Letters), ed. R. Lachower, 5 vols., Dvir, Tel Aviv, 1937–9. Letter for Adar 22nd., and Shereshevsky, *Rashi: The Man and his World*, p. 137.

2 I had myself a moving experience of this curiosity. One afternoon I entered an intermediate class in my Hebrew school where the students had been studying Genesis ch. 48. That chapter tells how Jacob persuaded his son Joseph to promise on oath that upon his (Jacob's) death Joseph would arrange to have his body taken for burial in the ancestral burial cave in the Holy Land. In the course of the conversation beween father and son, Jacob admits (verse 7) *And as for me when I came from Paddan, Rachel died unto me in the land of Canaan in the way . . . and I buried her there.* Now Rashi, commenting on the last phrase, says: 'And I did not even bring her into Bethlehem into the Holy Land. And I know that you have something against me because of that. But I want you to know that I buried her there on Divine instruction so that when, in the distant future, Nebuzaradan will drive the Jews into Babylonian exile, they will pass that way and Rachel will come out of her grave pleading mercy for her children as it is written, *A voice is heard in Ramah, lamentation and a bitter weeping, Rachel weeping for her children* (Jer. 31:15). And God will reply . . . *Thy work shall be rewarded. And they shall come back from the land of their enemy* (ibid., 16).' Now the teacher was an enthusiastic educator with a good voice, and he taught the class the Rashi commentary to a special chant which he remembered from his own childhood days in Poland. The interesting thing is that the biblical text was absorbed into the Rashi text so that the children

did not know which was the Bible text and which were the words of Rashi.

3 Fraenkel, *Darko shel Rashi Beferushav La-Talmud Ha-Bavli*, pp. 95–6.

4 See pp. 16–17.

5 Rashbam, commentary on Gen. 37:13.

6 Small pieces of parchment on which are written the two paragraphs of the Shema (Deut. 6:4–9; 11:13–21). The parchment is placed inside a cover which is then fixed to the door post of the house in accordance with the biblical law in those two paragraphs.

7 Small boxes in which are placed four paragraphs from the Bible containing the command to write the words of God as signs for the hand and the head. The usual translation of *tephillin* is 'phylacteries', a word from the Greek meaning 'amulet'. This is a misnomer since the Hebrew comes from a word connected with the meaning of prayer.

8 Interestingly, this is the order of the paragraphs found in an ancient pair of *tephillin* in a cave at Qumran, near the Dead Sea.

9 Neeman, *Rashi Mefaresh Hatorah*, p. 222 ff.

10 Commentary on Avoth.

11 In fact modern soft-cover editions of separate tractates are inexpensively published today and include most of the commentaries of the standard Vilna edition.

12 *The Pentateuch and Haftorahs*, ed. J. H. Hertz, London, 1936.

13 *The Soncino Books of the Bible*, ed. A. Cohen, London, 1945.

14 *The Torah, A Modern Commentary*, ed. Plaut, Bamberger and Hallo, U. A. H. C., New York, 1981.

15 The testimony of J. H. Hertz speaks for all other modern commentators. 'No other commentary on the Pentateuch has had a more enduring popularity or exerted an equal influence on Jewry.'

16 Published in separate volumes by The Institute for Talmudic Publications, Jerusalem. The work, which was started in 1967, is not yet completed.

17 Published by the United Synagogue of America, New York (1965). To date only a few random treatises have been published.

SELECT BIBLIOGRAPHY

Abrahams, Israel, *Jewish Life in the Middle Ages*, Jewish Publication Society of America, Philadelphia, 1896.

American Association of Jewish Research, *Rashi Anniversary Volume*, New York, 1940.

Berliner, Abraham, *Raschi, der Kommentar des Salamo B. Isak über den Pentateuch*, Frankfurt a.M., 1905.

Berliner, Abraham, *Kuntrus Ha-loazim* (Heb.), Cracow, 1905.

Blumenfield, Samuel M., *Master of Troyes*, Behrman House, New York, 1946.

Darmsteter, Arsène, *Les Glosses Françaises de Raschi*, Durlacher, Paris, 1909.

Efrati, M. Z., *Rashi, Chayav Umifalav*, (Heb.), Tel Aviv, 1957.

Elfcnbein, I. S., ed., *Rashi: His Teachings and Personality*, Jewish Agency, New York, 1958.

Elfenbein, I. S., *Teshuvot Rashi* (Heb.), New York, 1943.

Florsheim, Joel, *Rashi Lemikra Beferusho La-Talmud* (Heb.), Reuben Mass, Jerusalem, 1985.

Fraenkel, Jonah, *Darko shel Rashi Beferushav La-Talmud* (Heb.), Jerusalem, 1975.

Gordin, Abba, *Rashi* (Heb.), Massadah, Tel Aviv, 1961.

Graetz, Heinrich, *History of the Jews*, vols. III and IV, Jewish Publication Society of America, Philadelphia, 1895.

Heilperin, H., *Rashi and the Christian Scholars*, Pittsburgh University Press, 1963.

Landau, Moses, *Marpe Lashon* (Heb.), Odessa, 1865. On Rashi's foreign words.

Lauterbach, J. Z., *Rashi the Talmud Commentator*, Central Conference of American Rabbis, Cincinnati, 1940.

Liber, Maurice, tr. Adele Szold, *Rashi*, Jewish Publication Society of America, Philadelphia, 1948.

Maimon, Judah Leib, *Midei Hodesh Behodsho* (Heb.), vol. I, Mossad Harav Kook, Jerusalem, 1955.

Marx, Alexander, *Essays in Jewish Biography*, Jewish Publication Society of America, Philadelphia, 1947.

Neeman, Pinhas, *Rashi Mofaresh Hatorah* (Heb.), Massadah, Jerusalem, 1946.

Pearl, Chaim, *Rashi, Commentaries on the Pentateuch*, Viking Press, New York, 1970.

Rosenbaum, M., and Silbermann, A. M., *Pentateuch with Rashi's Commentary*, Hebrew Publishing Company, New York, 1934.

Schloesser, Max, *Rashi, His Life and Work*, Baltimore, 1905.

Shereshevsky, Ezra, *Rashi: The Man and his World*, Sepher-Hermon Press, New York, 1982.

Smalley, R., *The Study of the Bible in the Middle Ages*, University of Notre Dame, Indiana, 1964.

Waxman, M., *History of Jewish Literature*, Yoseloff, London and New York, 1960.

Zeitlin, Solomon, *Rashi*, in *American Jewish Year Book*, vol. 41, New York, 1939, pp. 111–140.

INDEX

Aaron, 23, 47
Abel, 38
Abrabanel, Isaac, 93
Academies
  in Babylon, 6, 66, 67
  in Mainz, 6
  in Palestine, 66
  in Troyes, 13, 15, 93
aggadah, 27, 39, 41, 42, 44, 45, 88,
  90, 99
Akiba, 86
Anan ben David, 29
Apostates, 14, 20, 101
Arabic, 30, 35
Aramaic, 34, 54, 55, 67, 68, 87,
  88
Avoth, tractate, 107
avoth nezikin, principle damages,
  80

Baba Batra, tractate, 16, 70
Baba Kama, tractate, 76, 78, 81,
  83
Baba Mezia, tractate, 75, 76, 79
Babel, tower of, 22, 46
Babylon, 5, 6, 18, 29, 68, 105
Babylonian exile, ix, 24, 106
baraita, 73, 83, 84
Bass, Shabbetai, 97
Berachoth, tractate, 72, 74, 103
Bereavement, 21
Bereshith Rabbah, 39, 48, 49,
  104
Bethlehem, 106

Bible exegesis, ix, 5, 25, 93, 99,
  100
Burial, on Intermediate Days of
  festivals, 20–21

Cain, 38
Caro, Joseph, 91
Chamber of Hewn Stones, see
  Lishkath Ha-gazith
Champagne, 8, 9
Charlemagne, 1
Charles VI, 101
Christians, 3, 11, 14, 22, 28, 48,
  58, 100
Chullin, tractate, 104
Church, 2, 3, 4, 14, 15, 27
crowns, to Torah letters, 86
Crusades, 1, 3, 5, 13–14, 15–16,
  48
Curses, Moses' eleven, 43

Derara demamona, 79
derush, 26, 27, 30, 38–45, 47–50,
  52–3, 55, 58, 62, 72, 96, 99
Donin, Nicholas, 101
Dunash ben Labrat, 35, 36
Duran, Simon ben Zemah, 97

Easter, 3
Eduyoth, tractate, 104
ed zomem, confuted witness, 85
Egypt, 31, 46, 61
Elhanan, Jewish pope, 102
Eliezer ben Yose, Rabbi, 24, 103